TOMSON HIGHWAY

Talonbooks
2003

Talonbooks
P.O. Box 2076, Vancouver, British Columbia, Canada V6B 3S3
www.talonbooks.com

Typeset in New Baskerville and printed and bound in Canada.

First Printing: October 2003

"Should Only Native Actors Have the Right to Play Native Roles" was
first published in *Prairie Fire*, Vol. 22, No. 3 (Autumn 2001): 20–26.

National Library of Canada Cataloguing in Publication Data

Highway, Tomson
  Rose / Tomson Highway.

  A play.
  ISBN 0-88922-490-0

  I. Title.
PS8565.I433R67 2003   C812'.54   C2003-910965-8

The publisher gratefully acknowledges the financial support of the
Canada Council for the Arts; the Government of Canada through the
Book Publishing Industry Development Program; and the Province
of British Columbia through the British Columbia Arts Council for
our publishing activities.

To the memory of, and in thanks to, a friend, an extraordinary dramaturge, and an even more extraordinary director, Larry Evan Lewis, 1964–1995. This script burns with the wisdom, the immense generosity, and the courage of your spirit. To the memory of a man who was never afraid of dreaming big. Igwani kwayus, niweecheewagan.

Acknowledgements

Rose started off as a cabaret of songs produced by Native Earth Performing Arts Inc. of Toronto, Ontario. Subsequently, the script was co-commissioned by the Manitoba Theatre Centre, the National Arts Centre and the Canadian Stage Company, where it was workshopped, as it was, just previous to that, by the PlayRites Colony, Banff Centre, Banff, Alberta. The author wishes to thank these organizations together with all the incredibly talented people who contributed to the various workshops, readings and performances—most especially the late Larry Lewis, director extraordinaire.

The world premiere, however, was most generously—and miraculously—accomplished by the University College Drama Programme, University College, University of Toronto, Toronto, Ontario on the night of January 31, 1999 under the guidance of two extraordinary women: Dr. Pia Kleber (Head of the University College Drama Programme), who was the producer, and Leah Cherniak, who was the director.

The creative team and cast for this first production was (in alphabetical order):

Lena Arabian:	PUSSY COMMANDA
David Brands:	FRITZ THE KATZ, LUCIANO BOCCIA
Alana Brascoupe:	ROSETTA DICTIONARY
Patricia Cano:	EMILY DICTIONARY
Yvonne Czerny:	GAZELLE NATAWAYS, HERA KEECHIGEESIK

Max Ingrao:	ZACHARY JEREMIAH KEECHIGEESIK, WOODEN INDIAN
Johanna McDonald:	LIZ JONES
Nicole Manek:	VERONIQUE ST. PIERRE
Hart Massey:	BIG JOEY
Kathy Mile:	PHILOMENA MOOSETAIL, JEALOUSY Y. COME AGAIN
Tom Osborne:	MUNCHOOS X. COME AGAIN
Jeff F. Pestell:	CREATURE NATAWAYS
Gray Powell:	PIERRE ST. PIERRE
Angie Ryan:	ANNIE COOK
Andrew Shaver:	LUCIANO'S BODYGUARD
Jeannette Sousa:	ROSABELLA JEAN BAEZ
Natalie West:	CHIEF BIG ROSE

PRODUCER:	Pia Kleber
DIRECTOR:	Leah Cherniak
MUSICAL DIRECTOR:	Allen Cole
SET & COSTUME DESIGNERS:	Astrid Janson, Natalie Aigner, Carol Camper, Emelie Changur, Janice Fraser, Ulf Otto, Kerry Segal, Shannon Strype, Elaine Young
LIGHTING DESIGNER:	Peter Freund
ASST. LIGHTING DESIGNER:	Paul Cegys
CHOREOGRAPHER:	Sally Lyons
DRAMATURGE:	Gerd Hauck
TECHNICAL DIRECTOR:	Peter Freund
ASST. TECHNICAL DIRECTOR:	Jonathan Parker

ASST. DIRECTORS:	Erin O'Reilly,
	Tom Osborne,
	Jonathan Parker,
	Andrew Shaver
STAGE MANAGER:	Kimberly Purtell
ASST. STAGE MANAGERS:	Claudio Chiodo,
	Caroline Devlin,
	Lina Falomkina,
	Lynn Willis
VOICE COACH:	Michael Connolly
PERCUSSIONIST:	Eli Cohen
GUITARIST:	David Brands
SAXOPHONIST:	Jeff F. Pestell

Production Notes

A great chunk of this play, it goes without saying, is illusion, theatrical sleight-of-hand—lights, sounds, music. And, of course, *acting*. What else, after all, is "theatre" about?

As impossible as it sounds to produce, that is to say, this show is still surprisingly do-able, as was proven most brilliantly—and daringly—by a brave, generous and shockingly imaginative producer named Pia Kleber of Toronto, Ontario and an equally brave, generous and shockingly imaginative director named Leah Cherniak, also of Toronto, together, of course, with the help of a wild and talented bunch of actors, designers, musicians, production crew and friends to die for. What they did, in the end—other, that is, than create an unforgettable theatrical experience for many, many people—was provide me, the playwright, with the highlight of my life in the theatre to date. What pleasure, what friendship, what love, what joy!

The question still begs, however: how on Earth did they do it? Well, for one thing, there *are no* motorcycles. I repeat: it is *all* illusion. Pardon me, there is *one* motorcycle. And it doesn't move, not on its own, not mechanically. That is to say: it need never be turned on, it shouldn't be—a moving motorcycle on stage would be too dangerous. Besides, motorcycles being driven on to the stage? Been done before. Boring. All that is needed, then, to create the effect of a legion of motorbikes—besides the one real motorcycle—is handlebars and head lights. *That's all.*

And in place of all things black leather such as jackets, vests and whatnot? Vinyl, of course, is the answer, or cheap Sally Ann issue black silk which, under low lighting, *can* look like black leather. All that is needed, after all—and to repeat yet again—is the *illusion* of black leather.

And the rest? When *objects* are mentioned in the script with quotation marks around them—e.g. "slot machines," "blackjack tables," "jukebox," "bed," "stove," etc.—that means these "objects" are purely *illusory*. The same goes for verbs like "floats." You don't need a real slot machine, a real jukebox, or a real stove; you don't need to make an actor "float" in air or water. Just pretend, just "mime" the idea. Or use a feather-weight styrofoam cube (or cubes). "Pretend." That is the operative word here as, come to think of it, should be the case with every play ever written. The word "acting," for instance. Isn't the meaning of the verb the following: that an *actor* is just *acting* at being—i.e. *pretending* to be—someone she/he is not?

My suggestion to anyone who puts on a show as a result of the above-named challenges and questions? Think of the exercise as just a bunch of kids, the kind *you* were when you were five years old, playing in and with a chest filled with old clothes and objects.

And last, the old—and very tiresome—question: "Should Only Native Actors Have the Right to Play Native Roles?" (Which to me has always sounded a lot like: "Should only Italian actors have the right to play Italian roles?" Or: "Thought Police Productions presents an All-German-Cast in *Mother Courage* by Bertold Brecht. Only Germans need apply.") Myself, I think the question looms large enough for it to merit an article all its own included in a publication such as this one, so it is, accordingly, at the end of this play. The question certainly affects, for one thing, the life, the livelihood, the income—the very physical survival—of at least one professional, practicing Native playwright. And I'm sorry but earning *money* as a playwright just to meet your rent beats, by a very long mile, living on welfare at the cost of the state, living on the street as a drunk, or rotting in a jail for beating your wife to death (*and*, in the process, eating up $40,000 *a year*, in some cases for a lifetime—for rent, food, clothing, supervision, healthcare, etc.—of taxpayers' very hard-earned money.

The Set

The set, for all intents and purposes, should be constructed roughly, and quite simply, as follows:

At extreme stage right is Emily's living room, represented simply by a tired old couch. At extreme stage left is Big Joey's basement, represented by an old motorcycle (which, of course, is initially covered with "motorcycle parts" and "biker chick mannequins" who, of course, come to life at play's opening, only to reveal the *real* motorcycle sitting there, in Big Joey's basement.). In between these two "power spots" is the Community Hall which, ultimately is just a higgledy-piggledy collection of chair-height styro-foam cubes which, perhaps, on one, two, or three sides, could be painted with the hearts and spades and clubs and diamonds and queens and jacks and kings of your standard deck of playing cards and, of course, can be moved, on a dime, by the actors so they serve, in an instant, as chairs, blackjack tables, slot machines, voting booths, whatever is needed as the play progresses. That is the main level of the stage.

High above that is a second level which, for all intents and purposes, will serve as the domain of "the gods" or, in this case, "goddesses." That is to say, it is the realm of "the tricksters," the home of "the Roses," denizens of the world of the spirit—together, of course, with their hearts which, in the end, are the moons that circle the planet we live on.

All other effects—the jukebox, for instance, and the roulette wheel—are achieved just with lighting sleight-of-hand. Theatre magic, as they say in the business.

And that, my friends, is it …

Cast of Characters

To be played by 17 actors, minimum, 10 female, 7 male:

The Women:

    EMILY DICTIONARY, 38 years old

    LIZ JONES, 36

    PUSSY COMMANDA, 35

    CHIEF BIG ROSE, 59

    ROSABELLA JEAN BAEZ, 38

    ROSETTA DICTIONARY, 5*

    GAZELLE NATAWAYS, 38

    VERONIQUE ST. PIERRE, 50

    PHILOMENA MOOSETAIL, 55

    ANNIE COOK, 42

    HERA KEECHIGEESIK, 39

    JEALOUSY Y. COME AGAIN, 40

The Men:

    BIG JOEY, 41

    CREATURE NATAWAYS, 41

    ZACHARY JEREMIAH KEECHIGEESIK, 41

    PIERRE ST. PIERRE, 55

    MUNCHOOS X. COME AGAIN, 45

    FRITZ THE KATZ, 45

    LUCIANO BOCCIA, 45

    LUCIANO'S BODYGUARD, 30

    ELVIS PRESLEY, 41 (*optional*)

    WOODEN INDIAN

… and at least 7 dancing avocado plants to be doubled, obviously, by actors playing the above-listed characters. Other suggested doubling: GAZELLE/HERA, PHILOMENA/ JEALOUSY, FRITZ/LUCIANO, ZACHARY/WOODEN INDIAN.

* (*NOTE: actor could be 8, 10, even 12, so long as she is physically small and could pass for 5 or thereabouts.*)

Time: March 1992 to October 1992

Place: The Wasaychigan Hill Indian Reserve, Manitoulin Island, Ontario

Songs (in order of performance):

Act One

Healing Chant—Emily
Tansi—the women
"Kisageetin" Means "I Love You"—Gazelle, Rosabella, Liz, Pussy
Tango—instrumental only
She Was a Doll—Emily, Liz, Pussy
Jukebox Lady—Rosabella, Emily (with Liz and Pussy)

Act Two

The Hilarium—Chief Big Rose with Emily, Gazelle, Liz, Pussy
Lookin' for Love—Emily, Liz, Pussy
Dance of Attack—instrumental only
Lookin' for Love—Emily, Liz, Pussy, Rosabella
Movin' Out, Movin' In—Company
When Children Sleep—Emily (with the women)

Act Three

Jukebox Lady—Emily, Liz, Pussy
The Place Where I Belong—Annie (with Emily, Liz, Gazelle and Company)
White Boys Fall in Love—Emily, Liz, Gazelle (and Company)
Tansi (reprise)—the women
When Children Sleep (lullaby only)—the women
Rio in High January—Liz, Emily, Pussy and Company
Tango (reprise)—instrumental only
The Thank You Song—Rosabella, Emily and Company

ACT ONE

First, in the darkness and the silence, a heartbeat,
then breathing.

Scene One: Emily's Living Room

Song(s): "Healing Chant" and "Tansi"

Early March, 1992, on the Wasaychigan Hill Indian
Reserve, Manitoulin Island, Ontario. The only light
comes from a full moon up in the night sky. Alone,
EMILY DICTIONARY kneels on her living room floor,
staring zombie-like into empty air. Then she begins to
weep. And to speak quietly, to herself.

EMILY

Taneegi? Taneegi pimatisiwin? Taneegi uwinuk kapima-
tisit? ("Why? What's the reason for living? I mean, why
bother?")

(The English translation of her lines plays, like an
echo, or a wind, on theatre sound system.) Slowly, she
rises, goes to a "drawer" and takes out of it an
unfinished piece of pink smocking (for a newborn
baby), one elegant red stiletto shoe and an eagle
feather, all three of which she holds tenderly in her
hands and then puts into a paper box which sits on
the counter. Then she takes from a cupboard a braid
of sweetgrass, a book of matches and a saucer. Then
she goes to squat on the floor in the middle of the

*room, puts the box and other materials down in front
of her and, rocking back and forth, begins to intone
quietly, as in prayer. She is praying.*

EMILY

Wee-chee-ik. Wee-chee-ik ooma keethawow, iga awasimee
eenootee-pimatisiyan, eenooteen-piyan, eenooteen-
paysooyan. Eewa? Peeweechee-ik seemak. Seemak.
Igatchee ... igatchee ... ("Help me. Help me all of you,
cuz I don't wanna live no more, cuz I wanna die, wanna
kill myself. Please? Come and help me, right away. Right
away. Or else ... or else ... ")

*(Again, the English translation of her lines—or at
least, parts thereof—plays, like an echo or a wind, on
theatre sound system.)*

*Lighting a match, she begins to chant a healing song.
Then she lights the sweetgrass and begins a ceremony
of purification. The "cabaret rhythm" of the song
"Tansi" begins to pulse, faintly, as if coming from
deep within the box at her knees. Then the box itself
begins to glow. With a flash of terror, EMILY grabs the
box, rushes to the "window," and throws it out.*

*ROSETTA DICTIONARY, a girl of 5, skips happily down
a "road." When four men who look vaguely like
Mafiosi appear in the shadows around her, ROSETTA
freezes in fear. But then she hears music pulsating
faintly from a box on the "dirt road." Drawn to it,
ROSETTA opens the box. And the music grows in
volume. The men stop and watch, as if waiting for
the right moment to grab her.*

*Entranced, ROSETTA reaches into the box and takes
out a doll that is the image of ROSABELLA JEAN BAEZ,
dressed in black leather and straddling a motorcycle.
Away upstage, seemingly hovering in empty air, an
old "jukebox" appears behind the coloured glass of
which sits the ghost of ROSABELLA JEAN BAEZ, a
goddess in black leather, straddling a motorcycle.
ROSETTA next brings out a doll that looks like CHIEF
BIG ROSE herself, also on a motorcycle, and, at down-*

stage centre, CHIEF BIG ROSE *herself appears. Wearing a pinkish, floral-pattern granny dress, black leather jacket and black leather police hat, and standing beside a "motorcycle,"* CHIEF BIG ROSE *holds her famous silver hammer in one hand, the text of a speech in the other as she practices this speech (wordlessly for now).* ROSETTA *last brings out a third biker doll that looks like herself, which she begins to "play-fly" in the air.*

A gunshot resounds, echoing three times. The three ROSES *freeze. Silence. The four shadowy men, handguns pointed, slowly begin to recede into the shadows and disappear. A pin spot comes up on the face of* EMILY DICTIONARY. *Sitting up from sleep, as from a nightmare,* EMILY *searches the room with her eyes, as though looking for a ghost.*

EMILY

(*With huge pain.*) Rose!!!

Through this next sequence, EMILY *remains deliberately uninvolved. At first, it sounds like wolves in the distance, howling at the moon. But it is actually women, lamenting, crying out, their Cree and English weaving in and out of each other.*

WOMEN

(*Off-stage.*) Igwani! Igwani eewaniya-ak kimisinow! Igwani eewaniya-ak kitoogimaminow! Tansi itigwee igwa paskutch keetootamak! Tansi itigwee igwa paskutch kee-tootamak! ... Lost! Lost! We have lost our sister! We have lost our dearly beloved Rose! What are we to do? Oh, what are we to do? ...

Behind ROSETTA, *lights slowly reveal a hill littered with reject "motorcycles" and "motorcycle parts" high over which "hovers" the old "jukebox" with the ghost of* ROSABELLA *behind it. Rosetta's toy box and the jukebox both emit puffs of smoke and, snapping back to life,* ROSABELLA *begins to sing.*

15

ROSABELLA

(*Singing.*) "Tansi, niweecheewaganuk, tansi,
Tapwee geechi kapeegee-oogeeyik;
Nimeetheeth'weeteenan tapapeeyak,
Tachimoostatak tanagamooyak … "

> *Also snapping back to life, CHIEF BIG ROSE and
> ROSETTA join ROSABELLA in her song as … Flanking
> ROSABELLA and leaning up against "motorcycles"
> appear LIZ JONES and PUSSY COMMANDA, wearing
> "black leather" shorts and halters, black net stockings
> and garter belts, black leather police hats. They too
> join in the song. From the middle of the heap of
> "motorcycles" then rise PHILOMENA MOOSETAIL and
> ANNIE COOK and, moments later, the exquisitely
> groomed JEALOUSY Y. COME AGAIN. All wear the
> trappings of their day-to-day lives, but with some
> mark that reads "motorcycle woman." Next to rise are
> HERA KEECHIGEESIK and VERONIQUE ST. PIERRE and
> then, between them, the incredible GAZELLE
> NATAWAYS, who wears a strapless pink sheath gown,
> black leather opera gloves, police hat, "diamonds"
> dripping, a long cigarette holder in one hand, a
> cat-o-nine tails whip in the other. All the women now
> singing, the entire trash heap becomes one pulsating,
> glorious vision in pink, black and silver. As though
> reading from the text in her hand, CHIEF BIG ROSE
> begins to speak, the instrumental section of the song
> continuing faintly in the background.*

CHIEF BIG ROSE

(*Speaking the words to the women's verse just above.*)
"Tansi, niweecheewaganuk, tansi,
Tapwee geechi kapeegee-oogeeyik;
Nimeetheeth'weeteenan tapapeeyak,
Tachimoostatak tanagamooyak … welcome, my friends,
welcome. How kind of you to come and visit us tonight.
Because we just love to laugh … " Nah, it sounds silly in
English. Maybe I should do it all in Cree. But then Bob
Rae won't understand a word I'm saying … "

WOMEN

(*Singing.*) "Astum, peetooteek, astum, peenasin,
Tachimoostatak, k'wayus kapapin;
K'wayus kikamama-skateenawow,
Kikamatoonawow, kika-papin ... "

> As the song crescendos to full volume, the women
> move towards CHIEF BIG ROSE, doing the traditional
> women's shawl dance in one long chorus-line across
> the downstage area. The men stalk them, making
> provocative sexual gestures. But the women look
> straight ahead, their dance dignified and stately. The
> men and the women recede into the shadows, the song
> growing fainter until only CHIEF BIG ROSE (other than
> EMILY, still frozen in the shadows) is left, centre-stage,
> alone in the Community Hall, still practicing her
> speech.

CHIEF BIG ROSE

(*Speaking the words to the women's song just above.*)
"Astum, peetooteek, astum, peenasin;
Tachimoostatak, k'wayus kapapin;
K'wayus kikamama-skateenawow,
Kikamatoonawow, kika-papin ... Come to us, approach
us, come, come to get us. We'll tell you stories, you will
laugh very hard, you will be astonished, you will cry, you
will ... " Ach, it still sounds stupid in English. So yes, I
think I'll do it all in Indian. After all, I don't give a hoot
whether the Premier of Ontario understands a word of
Cree or not, that's his problem, not ...

> Glass shatters. CHIEF BIG ROSE screams and whips
> around to look at a broken "window." Men's
> taunting voices can be heard outside, receding into
> the distance. CHIEF BIG ROSE looks out the "window."

CHIEF BIG ROSE

(*Under her breath.*) Bastards.

> Fade-out. As, high up above, an Indian chief
> headdress floats across, CHIEF BIG ROSE following it
> with puzzled eyes.

Scene Two: The Community Hall

Song: "The Thank You Song" (hummed only)

*That afternoon, at the Community Hall, the
Homemakers' Club is in session, working on Indian
chief headdresses. HERA finishes sweeping broken
"glass" into a dust pan, then goes to join PHILOMENA
and VERONIQUE who are working on patterns for pow
wow dancing bustles. The women hum "The Thank
You Song."*

CHIEF BIG ROSE

Them mangy curs. I wiped the shit from off their naked
bums when they were but babes in their mothers' arms
and what do they do to thank me? Six this morning, a
knock comes on my door, I open it, and there's a fire on
my step so I stomp it out and what do I get? A bedroom
slipper covered in shit. Some monkey went and filled a
paper bag with shit, left it on my porch, set it on fire, and
stood back like a spineless coward to watch me stomp it
out and get my bedroom slipper covered in … shit.

PHILOMENA

Pelajia Rosella Patchnose? A woman trying to run a Band
Council made up of men who think women were born to
give birth, wash dishes, eat chocolates and watch soap
opera is asking for …

CHIEF BIG ROSE

You, Philomena Moosetail, may still be living in the stone
age but I am strictly a twentieth-century woman so
women washing dishes, watching soap opera, pooh! Left
that crap behind me years ago, now take this Indian chief
headdress, for instance. Did you, as recently as ten years
ago, ever think that a woman would dare to wear such a
thing?

PHILOMENA

No, but people around here? Especially the men? They
will be shocked.

CHIEF BIG ROSE
Too damn bad.

HERA
I thought that headdress was for The Honourable Mr.
Bob Rae.

CHIEF BIG ROSE
Hera Keechigeesik? We're doing mine first. Bob's can
wait.

VERONIQUE
You're going to put an Indian chief headdress on Bob
Rae's head?

PHILOMENA
Imagine. The *Premiere* of the province of Ontario coming
to *le pauvre* Wasaychigan Hill.

CHIEF BIG ROSE
And why not, Philomena Moosetail?

HERA
When's that humourless old thing supposed to get here
anyway?

VERONIQUE
Friday, the third of July, 1992, at 1:45 p.m.

PHILOMENA
(*A sensual revel.*) Woomph!

CHIEF BIG ROSE
Woomph, yourself, because one good dose of my robust
and meaty sense of humour and Bob Rae's life will never
be the same.

VERONIQUE
Mary Mother of Jesus, I wish I had a new stove so I could
roast him the biggest roast beef à la chipoocheech that
has been roasted on this reserve since the day …

CHIEF BIG ROSE
Fortunately for him, Veronique St. Pierre, all he has to do
is sign the agreement giving the land under the township
of Manitowaning …

VERONIQUE

... which they stole from the Indians a century ago ...

CHIEF BIG ROSE

... back to the Indians, have his picture taken with me plunking a headdress on his head, thus crowning him Chief Brown Bear, then he's off with his motorcade.

PHILOMENA

Premiere Bob Rae has a motor-*cad?*

HERA

Of course, he does, he's the Premier of Ontario, is he not. Then again, if this *Premiere* Bob is coming to Wasaychigan Hill with a motor-*cad* behind him, then don't you think *our* chief should meet him with ...

PHILOMENA

... her own motor-*cad?* (*HERA nods at her.*) Imagine. *My* sister, Pelajia Rosella Patchnose with her own ...

VERONIQUE

Don't make me chortle.(*Chortles anyway.*) Zxzyxzyxzyx!

Hearing ANNIE COOK's rapid signature rhythm heralding her approach, PHILOMENA peeks out a "window."

PHILOMENA

Why, I do believe that cloud of dust roaring up the hill is Annie Cook, Pelajia, and she's looking madder than a mink in a pot.

VERONIQUE

That little minx was singing at Big Joey's Juke Joint— again—till five this morning, Black Lady Halked was telling me.

HERA

Ran out of country songs at four a.m. so started singing hymns, is what I heard.

VERONIQUE

(*Rushing to beat ANNIE to the punch.*) I promised Black Lady Halked I wouldn't tell a soul but her second cousin Teardrop Manigitogan told her she overheard Creature

Nataways' first cousin Black Eye Kananakeesik telling
June Bug McLeod ...

ANNIE

(*Off-stage.*) Ha-looo!

VERONIQUE

(*Now* really *rushing.*) ... that Big Joey has plans to expand
that little casino operation in his basement right here
into this Community Hall that we the ladies of the
Wasaychigan Hill Indian Reserve Homemakers' Club use
for our many useful activities such as preparing our Chief
for Premier Bob's first visit to ...

ANNIE

(*Zooming in.*) Pisses me off, treating Fritz the Katz like an
oom-chi-cha machine. Fritz the Katz is an artist, a professional.

CHIEF BIG ROSE

Annie Cook, is it true Big Joey has his eye on our
Community Hall for this ... this gambling operation of
his?

ANNIE

I don't know. But it's true. Big Joey needs something
bigger, something better, he needs to make more
money ...

HERA

Money, money, money ...

ANNIE

Yeah! He can't even pay Fritz the Katz.

CHIEF BIG ROSE

And the only bigger place available to the great man is
this hall?

ANNIE

I guess so, I don't know.

CHIEF BIG ROSE

This hall, Annie Cook, belongs to the Band Council.

VERONIQUE

Oh, I wouldn't put it past Big Joey to find some way of seducing one of those three anti-Come Again women on the Band Council right into his smelly, sweaty bed, whispering succulent blandishments into her ear and boom! Next thing you know, this Community Hall will be just sizzling and bubbling with criminals, prostitutes, drug dealers, bootleggers, strippers and gangsters.

CHIEF BIG ROSE

And knowing that mangy cur, we will have to act now, today, boom! Or the Wasaychigan Hill Indian Reserve Homemakers' Club will be homeless as a dead mink faster than you can say ... (*Searches for the word.*)

HERA

(*Coming to the rescue.*) ... Bob Rae.

Blackout.

Scene Three: Emily's, Big Joey's Basement, Toronto Bus Station, The Bus, Emily's

Song: "'Kisageetin' Means 'I Love You'"

In the darkness, a telephone rings. EMILY DICTIONARY finally breaks out of her freeze/trance and turns to look at it. Afraid to answer it, she lets it ring. And ring and ring. Fade-out.

Out of this darkness emerges the sensuous, femme fatale voice of GAZELLE NATAWAYS singing along to a "radio" that is playing sentimental jazz. As well, we hear BIG JOEY's voice reciting numbers like someone intoning the rosary.

BIG JOEY

(*Speaking, in the dark.*) ... 2,349; 1,567; 4,761; 879; 5,132 ...

GAZELLE

(*Singing, in the dark.*)
"Take me to the place where sunny days,

22

Just never cease to come your way,
And ocean breezes gently blow,
Or so I've heard men say ... "

> *Under* GAZELLE'*s song, the deep, honeyed voice of her*
> *man,* BIG JOEY, *comes rumbling out.*

BIG JOEY
(*Speaking, in the dark.*) California. Hmph.

> *Lights up on a bra draped over the seat of a*
> *motorcycle in Big Joey's basement. Instrumental of the*
> *song keeps playing "underneath" the dialogue that*
> *follows.*

GAZELLE
California?

BIG JOEY
Best slot machines on the market. Heck, if Munchoos X.
hadna brought me these catalogues, I woulda ended up
stopping in Nevada and paying twice as much.

> BIG JOEY *himself lies naked on a chaise longue, a*
> *catalogue to his eyes, a calculator on his mighty chest.*
> *Barely wearing a pink negligee, a glass of wine to her*
> *lips,* GAZELLE NATAWAYS *lies draped around* BIG
> JOEY*'s huge muscular thighs, utterly obsessed with*
> *him. Euphoric from drinking, gambling and then*
> *making love all night the night before, their clothes lie*
> *strewn everywhere in this after-hours-club-cum-casino.*

GAZELLE
Mmmmm so when are we going?

BIG JOEY
(*Working the calculator.*) ... 2,345; 3,455; 3,521 ...

GAZELLE
Pooch? When are we going?

> *Being the kind of guy who can be devastatingly*
> *charming when he wants,* BIG JOEY *says this next*
> *with gentle, playful impatience.*

BIG JOEY

Gazelle? Baby? I gotta have this budget ready for
Munchoos X. by tonight, okay?

*GAZELLE melts, turns away, and resumes singing
along to the "radio" as BIG JOEY calculates away.*

BIG JOEY

... 3,456; 6,238; 5,317 ...

GAZELLE

(*Singing.*) "They say California is a dream,
Where livin' high and all that jazz,
Just come to you so na-chur-lee,
As though they always wazz ... "

BIG JOEY

... 645; 2,389; 6,132 ...

*Fade-out ... though the music (instrumental only)
continues in the background.*

*At Emily's, the telephone rings. She turns to it again.
Way up above her, as though hovering in empty air, a
pair of shocking-red six-inch stiletto-heeled shoes
appears. Then the ghost of ROSABELLA JEAN BAEZ
appears next to them, sitting at her "dresser mirror"
in her "dressing room" languidly pulling on a nylon
stocking as she gets ready for "a show" for "the girls"
at "The Black Cat Soirée" (a nightclub in San
Francisco). A glass of wine sits in front of her, an
almost full wine bottle beside it. GAZELLE's song now
has a ghostly source, as ROSABELLA takes it over.*

ROSABELLA

(*Singing.*) "We'll take ourselves a little stroll,
Upon a beach, upon a golden shore,
We'll hold each other tender-lee,
Like no one else before ... "

The phone keeps ringing, EMILY finally answers it.

EMILY

(*Grouchy, on phone.*) Yeah, who is it?

*Lights reveal LIZ JONES and PUSSY COMMANDA with
luggage, standing at a "wall phone" in the Toronto
Bus Terminal. Away up in the air, ROSABELLA begins
putting on her other nylon stocking. Her wine glass is
now empty. From here on, she will get progressively
drunker.*

LIZ

(*On phone.*) I don't believe it, I don't fuckin' believe it,
Emily Dictionary, you old dyke you ...

PUSSY

(*Shouting into phone past LIZ's ear.*) Hi, Em!

LIZ

(*Mock angry.*) Puss! My ear! (*Back on phone.*) Emily, this is
a ghost from your ancient/ ... ancient past. Me and Puss,
we're in *Toronto* ... (*Shouts into phone.*) ... Toronto Bus
Terminal! ... and we ... (*Off phone.*) Damn!

PUSSY

(*Shouting into phone past LIZ's ear.*) /It's me, Em!
Remember me? Pussy Commanda? Pussy-you-wanna-
touch-it-you-wanna-squeeze-it-Commanda? (*Brilliant peal
of laughter.*)

LIZ

Puss, you got any more change on you hurry up hurry up
hurry up ...

EMILY

(*Covering mouthpiece.*) Oh, my god ...

*Fade-out as, high above, ROSABELLA JEAN BAEZ,
pouring herself another glass of wine, smiles down at
EMILY and then snaps a frilly black garter belt into
place.*

*Back to Big Joey's basement, where the "radio" is still
softly playing the instrumental to "'Kisageetin' Means
'I Love You,'" GAZELLE is now modelling a
bedsheet/toga in a "mirror."*

BIG JOEY

(*To himself.*) Slot machines 90,495, blackjack tables 9,979, lighting equipment 34,037 ... bringing my grand total up to ... 514,237 dollars!

GAZELLE

(*To herself, in the "mirror."*) Los Angeles. Gazelle Delphina Nataways. Rodeo Drive. Shopping.

BIG JOEY

Opening night! Friday, July third, 1992! Big Joey's "Island of Gold Casino Royale!" Ha-ha!

GAZELLE

... oooo my dream dress for that night? Satin ...

BIG JOEY

Old Chiefie wants economic development? Old Chiefie's gonna *get* economic development ...

GAZELLE

... *miles* of satin ...

BIG JOEY

Cuz this casino idea of mine? Within one year ... *one* ...

GAZELLE

... swishing thisaway and thataway and thisaway as I walk and when I turn?—"Oh! Somebody call me?"—it goes: "woosh!" Bodice. Tight.

BIG JOEY

... will be pumping a million dollars a year, easy, right into this reserve's bank account ...

GAZELLE

Cleavage that will slay every man who comes my way ...

BIG JOEY

... quite aside from shoving the unemployment figure from seventy-five percent right down ...

GAZELLE

... back naked as the night, right down ...

BIG JOEY

... down ...

GAZELLE

... to my crack ...

BIG JOEY

... down ...

GAZELLE

... of dawn. Diamonds, diamonds, and more diamonds, even here ...

BIG JOEY

... down ...

GAZELLE

... right across my fair ...

BIG JOEY

... to zero point zero zero zero zero ...

GAZELLE

... jeedeesh.

BIG JOEY

100, 200, 500, 1,000, 10,000 men—and women—all working for Joseph Jeremiah McLeod.

GAZELLE

(*Singing.*) "Then we'll pause to look out at the sea,
And revel in the silver spray
We'll frolic in an ocean wave,
The Californian way ... "

> *BIG JOEY turns a "slot machine" on and rams it into action. Fade-out as the instrumental of "Kisageetin ... " pulses on.*

> *EMILY can still be seen by her phone, ROSABELLA hovering above, now brushing her hair, her focus on EMILY. LIZ and PUSSY, meanwhile, sit on a travelling "Greyhound bus."*

PUSSY

(*Long silence.*) So. Should we?

LIZ

Should we what?

PUSSY

Bring up the topic of ... you know ... right off the top?

LIZ

Uh-uh. I don't want her closing up on us ...

PUSSY

Well, I think we should just get it over and done with.

LIZ

Puss, we're up here for one whole month. We've got plen ...

PUSSY

You practically went and forced Hortensia Colorado and the girls into this memorial ride to the fabulously dead and departed Rosabella Jean Baez. I mean, we all loved her dearly, Rose was a great woman but she wasn't God ...

LIZ

Emily thought she was.

PUSSY

Alright, alright. Night of Friday, July 3rd, 1992, Seven years to the day after the fact, twenty-one of us Indian women, less one, will be riding our bikes down the coast highway to the spot where Rose went and killed herself, let's just get it over with, let's just let the woman be dead and ...

LIZ

(*Firmly.*) She is *not* dead. Rosabella Jean Baez is not dead until Emily Dictionary—*and* the Rez Sisters—lay her spirit down to rest.

> *Finished with her hair,* ROSABELLA *starts on her fingernails as she sings to* EMILY *down below, the song now assuming the rhythm of a travelling bus.*

ROSABELLA

(*Singing.*) "Then I'll lay you down close by my side,
Upon that soft and silken sand,
And thus I will remind you that,
I'm yours forever and ... "

*For the last statement of the "chorus" to the song, LIZ
and PUSSY—from their "seats" on the night-travelling
"Greyhound bus"—join in with soft harmonies and
words. And GAZELLE, from her position leaning
languorously against the seat of the motorcycle in "the
basement" looking with desire at BIG JOEY, sings
along to ROSABELLA who's voice, ostensibly, is coming
from the "radio."*

ROSABELLA/GAZELLE
(*Singing: ROSABELLA to EMILY, GAZELLE to BIG JOEY*).
"'Kisageetin' means 'I love you,'
One simple word, one simple gift for you;
'Kisageetin, kisageetin,' that's all it means,
'I love you.'"

LIZ/PUSSY
(*Singing, as backup to above.*) "By the time we get to,
By the time we get to,
Get to Espanola,
She'll be fine;
By the time we
Get to Espanola,
Ahhh, ooooo … "

*As the light on LIZ and PUSSY fades, EMILY drops the
phone. Downing another glass of wine, ROSABELLA
blows EMILY a kiss and vanishes into a puff of smoke,
the red stiletto shoes on her dresser glinting magically
one last time in the moonlight.*

*Only Big Joey's basement remains lit, BIG JOEY and
GAZELLE now necking madly up against the
motorcycle.*

GAZELLE
… mmmphmmm so succulent, so juicy …

*The "door" bursts open and CREATURE NATAWAYS
falls into the room.*

CREATURE
Damn!

GAZELLE
Creature Nataways! Get out of here! Go on! Shoo!

CREATURE
That bottom step's gonna kill somebody someday, Big Joey, you gotta get it fixed, I tole you once I tole you twice, this place is falling apart it's too damn small for an operation like this, you gotta move to that Community Hall. Soon! So's you can get bigger bands, better ones too, than that ... that third rate piece of crap Fritz the Katz calls a ...

BIG JOEY
Fritz the Katz is fine for my basement. Them bigger bands, they come later.

CREATURE
Yeah, but Fritz the Katz is all up in arms, Big Joey, fact he may not show up at all tonight.

BIG JOEY
I'll deal with that has-been when he gets here. You get to work, go on, clean her up. (*To GAZELLE.*) Babe, shoot me them pants, will ya?

GAZELLE throws BIG JOEY his pants. Blackout.

Scene Four: Emily's Living Room

Song(s): "Lookin' For Love" (a capella) and "The Thank You Song" (one line only)

At Emily's, LIZ JONES and PUSSY COMMANDA stand at the "door" facing EMILY.

LIZ/PUSSY
(*Singing, in jazz harmony.*) "How are you, Emily? Emily, how are you?"

LIZ, PUSSY and EMILY hug each other intensely.

EMILY
(*Thrilled.*) Do it again.

LIZ

With you. Ready? (*EMILY and PUSSY nod.*) Un, deux.

EMILY/LIZ/PUSSY

(*Singing, in three-part jazz harmony.*) "How are you, Emily?
Emily, how are you?" (*They scream like little girls.*)

EMILY

Pure as the "p'sowgn" of a virgin. Hey. Remember this?

PUSSY

So, how come you never answered my letters?

EMILY

(*Snapping fingers and singing à la Peggy Lee's "Fever"*). "I'm
takin' a stroll, through the hot streets of town ... "

PUSSY

Aw, that one was the best ...

EMILY/PUSSY

(*Singing.*) "Well, it's high July, and the sun's beamin'
down; I'm searchin' for feelings, that I hope will be fine
... "

EMILY

(*Talking through the singing.*) Come on, Liz.

LIZ

I don't remember the words.

EMILY

Bullshit. You wrote 'em.

EMILY/PUSSY

(*Singing.*) "I'm lookin' at the people, I'm lookin' all
around me, God, I'm lookin' for love, God I'm lookin'
for love, God, I'm lookin' for, lookin' at the people ... "

EMILY

(*Speaking.*) Un, deux.

EMILY/LIZ/PUSSY

(*Singing, in jazz harmony.*) " ... and I'm lookin' for love ... "

EMILY

Remember when Hortensia Colorado used to go ... (*Like
the drum rolls in a song like "Fever."*) ... "poom, poom,
poom, prrrroom, poom ... "

31

PUSSY

(*Continuing in the background.*) Poom, poom, poom, prrrroom, poom …

EMILY

How *is* Hortensia?

LIZ

She's alright. Works in an abattoir.

PUSSY

With us poom, poom, prrrroom, poom … (*Continues in the background.*)

LIZ

Slaughterhouse. Meat. She can't wait to see you again. Insists you come back to San Fran with us.

EMILY

Is she still, like, is she still … riding?

PUSSY

(*Stops "poom, poom's."*) Nope. Whole gang broke up after the …

An uncomfortable silence, the mood of giddy happiness suddenly supplanted by excruciating discomfort.

PUSSY

… scattered to the … four winds. Like so much … sand. We all just got rid of our bikes, kissed each other good-bye, and … (*Searing silence.*)

LIZ

(*To EMILY.*) Why did you take off on us like that? (*Silence.*) Just ride off, disappear into the night without so much as one look back, no goodbye, nothing? (*Silence.*) Emily? (*Silence.*)

EMILY

(*With huge pain.*) How do you talk about something like that? (*Silence.*) Fucking goddamn stupid thing to go and do to your best friend. Selfish. Self-centred. Uncaring. There you are riding along beside her, the human being closest to your heart, when she rams her motorcycle into this 18-wheeler, blows herself to bits and you're right there beside her feeling her blood spraying all over the highway.

PUSSY

You sound pretty ... mad, Em, it's been ... a long time.

EMILY

Damn rights, I'm mad. Even after one hundred years, I'd still be mad at her. I'm angry at Rose, I'm pissed off as hell at Rosabella Jean Baez and I am never, ever going to forgive her for what she did to me that night so long as I live and breathe. (*Silence.*)

PUSSY

(*Nervously trying to melt the tension.*) "Poom, poom, poom, prrroom, poom ... " (*Continues under next two lines.*)

ANNIE

(*Off-stage.*) Ha-loooo!

LIZ

(*Singing, also trying to melt the tension.*) "Well, night's comin' on, city lights burnin' bright ... "

LIZ/PUSSY

"Still, I'm walking alone, and I ain't feelin' right ... "

The "door" opens and CHIEF BIG ROSE enters, followed by PHILOMENA, HERA, VERONIQUE and ANNIE, all trying to talk at once.

VERONIQUE/

It's everyone's business, absolutely everyone's ...

/PHILOMENA

What am I doing here? I should be home taking a bath ...

/HERA

I should have brought tobacco to offer Emily ...

/ANNIE

(*Singing, feigning Brenda Lee's voice in her song, "I'm Sorry."*) " ... so sorry, that love could be so cruel ... "

CHIEF BIG ROSE

Shush! (*Silence. CHIEF BIG ROSE pins EMILY with a glare. Everyone crowds around EMILY.*) You. Play the one-armed bandit, do you not?

EMILY

(*Puzzled.*) No. Can't say that I have.

CHIEF BIG ROSE

You. Play the blackjack, do you not?

EMILY

Nope. Don't know a thing about it.

CHIEF BIG ROSE

You. Could *learn* to play the blackjack, could you not?

EMILY

Get to the point. What do you want from me?

CHIEF BIG ROSE

You. Are the only woman around here who has the guts to stand up to Big Joey, are you not? (*Silence. EMILY merely looks back at CHIEF BIG ROSE.*) Good. So I'm asking you to sneak into that little basement casino of his, sniff out what he's up to, how ... In other words, Emily Dictionary, I'm asking you to become ... a spy. (*Suddenly sees LIZ and PUSSY.*) Hup! Who are these people? They look like they might make good ... spies.

LIZ

(*Offering her hand to CHIEF BIG ROSE.*) Liz Jones. Dyke.

PUSSY

(*To LIZ, witheringly.*) Meow. (*Then to CHIEF BIG ROSE.*) Pussy Commanda. Straighter than a two-by-four. San Francisco, California.

CHIEF BIG ROSE

Hmph. So tell me. Have you ever? Spied? On a man?

PUSSY

Well, I never thought of it quite that way but now that you mention it ...

LIZ and PUSSY look at each other and almost laugh.

PUSSY/LIZ

... yes ...

LIZ

... I guess ...

PUSSY/LIZ

... we have. (*They burst out laughing.*)

EMILY

(*To CHIEF BIG ROSE.*) *You?* Are asking *me?* To go to Big
Joey's?

HERA/

Emily, it seems there are certain people out there who ...

/VERONIQUE

... Vice-Chief Munchoos X. Come Again can't get used
to playing second fiddle after having been chief of this
reserve himself for the past eighteen years ...

/HERA

... certain people who don't appreciate the way Chief Big
Rose is going around making changes ...

/CHIEF BIG ROSE

... and I don't like it. Emily, when you first come into
this world, Mama left it. It was me took over caring for
you. Changed your diapers, fed you porridge, taught you
your alphabets, your numbers, your "Hail Mary's," raised
you straight into your teens when you take off with that
Dogrib piece a shit from Yellowknife and never come
home for near on sixteen years. No letter, not even a
postcard when my dear husband Joe Patchnose upped
and died from smoking too many of them damn
cigarettes. You show up on my doorstep and what do I
do? Open my arms real wide and receive you into 'em
like Mama would have done. And now I'm asking you for
help. You got a problem with that?

EMILY

Sorry. Ain't going nowhere near no asshole house. And
you all know the reason.

PUSSY

Emily.

EMILY

(*To PUSSY.*) Mind your own business, why don't you. Coming here, kicking up a whole lotta shit I been working like hell to forget.

VERONIQUE

Shame on you!

EMILY

Leave me alone, just fucking leave me alone. (*Starts pushing the women out.*)

CHIEF BIG ROSE

Watch your language!

EMILY

Go on, get out of here.

HERA

(*Stopping EMILY firmly.*) Emily, we are getting mighty damn tired of being treated like so much meat by these men. We want you to help us put a stop to it. For Chief Big Rose. For all of us.

> *EMILY is cornered. Hearing someone fall just outside the "window" on one side of Emily's living room, the women all turn towards it.*

MAN

(*Off-stage.*) You idiot! I told you not to let go.

> *Two men can be heard suppressing laughter and running off. Fade-out, during which ROSABELLA BAEZ can be heard singing (a line from "The Thank You Song") just outside the "window" on the opposite side of the room.*

ROSABELLA

(*Singing, off-stage.*) "When love ceases to exist … "

> *Spooked, EMILY snaps her head towards this "window," the only one in the room to have heard this voice. But only a gust of "wind" billows the "curtain" out.*

Scene Five: Big Joey's Basement

Song(s): "I'm Thinkin' of You" (intro. only), "Tango" and "She Was a Doll"

A Big Joey's Juke Joint. The "slot machines" in full swing, the room is filled with the sound of money falling into pails. Alone on stage, ANNIE COOK is adjusting the oom-chi-cha machine (i.e. one of those cheap automatic, push-button, electric keyboards) so it will play the instrumental tracks to the song, "I'm Thinkin' of You." Fritz the Katz's band instruments sit on the little stage behind ANNIE, FRITZ himself working a slot machine. CREATURE NATAWAYS is scurrying around nervously keeping things in order while BIG JOEY and PIERRE ST. PIERRE sit at a little lounge table in the foreground. Behind them, as the scene progresses, "gamblers" enter to play.

PIERRE
   … you see, if it wasn't for Munchoos X. Come Again and his wife Jealousy, I would have had only 124 votes …

BIG JOEY
   … Pierre …

PIERRE
   … now I can forget about the election of Pelajia Rosella Patchnose to the chiefdom of the Wasaychigan Hill Indian Reserve. I can forget about the election of Pierre St. Pierre to the Band Council of ye old same reserve but, holy shit la marde …

BIG JOEY
   … Pierre …

CREATURE
   (*Runs up.*) … you think he's gonna show up, huh, Big Joey? You think he's really gonna come tonight? … (*Runs off.*)

PIERRE

(*Ramming right through.*) … I will never, never so long as I'm alive and walking these dirt roads, ever forget the party Jealousy Y. Come Again threw the night before the big election. Broken champagne glasses all over creation, people dancing until they ended up in the basement because the floor finally caved in, women just a-peeling them leopard-skin coats from off their naked shoulders, even Jealousy Y. Come Again's two big fat Dalmation bitches were drunker than a pair of skunks in heat and dancing until they dropped dead …

BIG JOEY

Pierre, will you shut that trap of yours for just one goddamn minute?

CREATURE

(*Runs up.*) … It's getting mighty late, Big Joey, what if he doesn't show up? … (*Runs off.*)

PIERRE

… so the very next day, which was election day, people was so hung over, they didn't know which away they was a-voting so when the name of Pierre St. Pierre come up on the floor, people thought it was the name of Pierre Peter Papanikas they were hearing and that's the name they voted for and that's how I got into the Band Council and you can thank Jealousy Y. Come Again and her partying ways for that.

> BIG JOEY *takes three beers from under the table and bangs them down in front of PIERRE, pleasantly surprising the crazy old man.*

PIERRE

Tank you.

> *In one gulp, PIERRE downs a bottle and reaches for a second.*

BIG JOEY

There's twenty-one people on that Band Council, are there not?

PIERRE

Uh-huh?

BIG JOEY

And of those twenty-one people, ten are of the Come Again persuasion, are they not?

PIERRE

(*Bitter.*) Bah. Come Again, Schmum Again.

BIG JOEY

And you yourself are of the Come Again persuasion, are you not?

PIERRE

Well, as I say to anyone who cares to ask, I am and I am not.

BIG JOEY

Well, you can only be one way, you can't be both. Now come on, which is it?

> *Finishing his second beer, PIERRE bangs the bottle down on the table. For one fleeting second, the ghost of ROSABELLA BAEZ appears high above. Still at her dresser"mirror," she is now applying mascara to her eyes, the wine bottle beside her now almost empty. Just as ANNIE opens her mouth to sing "I'm Thinkin' of You," ROSABELLA, with the sweep of a hand, "commands" Annie's oom-chi-cha machine to change tracks and a tango begins to play, all by itself. Freaking out, ANNIE runs around turning this and that knob trying to get the machine to get back on track. BIG JOEY glares at ANNIE and is about to get up to tell her to shut up when PIERRE, as he talks, grabs him by the sleeve and forces him back down to his seat. The music becomes so infectious that PIERRE starts sort of "singing-speaking" his speech over the tango rhythm.*

PIERRE

My great grandfather, Lapatak St. Pierre, was married to a terrible woman whose name was Maskimoot Come Again but Maskimoot Come Again never had no babies on account of she was one of them virgin saints and then … (*Starts to sing.*) Maskimoot Come Again went and got trampled to death at the bingo, crushed, pfft! And so Lapatak St. Pierre went and married this other woman whose name was Prejudice Kananakeesik who is the woman who gave birth to my own grandpa, Salamoo St. Pierre and that's as far as my Come Again connection goes chikaboom chikaboom chikaboom, hey!

Finished with eye make-up, ROSABELLA toasts herself in her "mirror" with another glass of wine and "commands" the tango music to end, right on PIERRE's "hey!" which, again, knocks ANNIE COOK for a loop. BIG JOEY glares at her. In the background, MUNCHOOS X. COME AGAIN enters with, on his arm, his luxuriously dressed wife, JEALOUSY Y.; in fact, JEALOUSY is so beautiful (in a plastic, overly-made-up sort of way, with at least three face lifts so that her smile is permanent and motionless) that he "wears" her on his arm more for "decorative" purposes than for the fact that she happens to be human and his wife.

BIG JOEY

(*To PIERRE.*) So what's your problem with the Come Again clan, Pierre St. Pierre?

As the COME AGAINS gradually make their way to BIG JOEY's table, CREATURE excitedly scurries up to BIG JOEY to herald their arrival when PIERRE, unawares, makes a huge faux pas.

PIERRE

(*Loud.*) Jealousy Y. Come Again is a goddamn bitch, I'm sorry to announce.

CREATURE stops dead in his tracks and, wide-eyed, with horror, looks up at MUNCHOOS X. and JEALOUSY Y. who now stand immediately behind PIERRE. Then he gingerly tip-toes off to hide in the "crowd" while BIG JOEY smiles wickedly at PIERRE.

BIG JOEY

I thought you said you were grateful to Jealousy Y. for her partying ways.

Now applying lipstick, ROSABELLA "changes" ANNIE COOK's keyboard again. The tango resumes. ANNIE jumps off the stage and runs up to FRITZ, who has just entered, to CREATURE's relief.

ANNIE

Fritz.

FRITZ

Get off that stage, ya fucking scab..

Preoccupied with a "slot machine," FRITZ ignores her and she runs back to the stage to bite her nails and stare at the oom-chi-cha machine. Meanwhile, PIERRE rams on, still completely unaware that the COME AGAINS are standing right behind him.

PIERRE

Jealousy Y. Come Again talks backwards at me every chance she gets. Like, for instance, not two days ago, she calls me up and asks me if I plan to vote thisaway or that-away on this whole casino brouhaha and when I told her I was voting thisaway only if Munchoos X. Come Again promised me the Come Again clan would share just a little bit of them casino profits with the St. Pierre clan, she hung up in my face … (*Starts to sing.*) … and next thing you know, Jealousy Y. Come Again is running up and down Wasaychigan Hill telling every Tom, Harry and Big Dick that Pierre St. Pierre is an S.O.B. for accusing Munchoos X. Come Again of stabbing Chief Big Rose in the back on account of this casino idea of yours, Big Joey, holy shit la marde, I just about ate my shorts, but you see I already know that Munchoos X. Come Again and all them greedy guts Come Again types are putting thousands of dollars of their own money into this casino idea of yours and I already know that when this new casino opens—if it opens—it may belong to the people of Wasaychigan Hill, on paper, yes, but in the bank, it will belong to you and Munchoos X. Come Again and you wanna know how I know that? Why, you yourself said …

BIG JOEY

(*At MUNCHOOS over PIERRE's shoulder.*) Chikaboom chikaboom chikaboom, hey!

Now putting on an earring, ROSABELLA changes the electric keyboard back to normal. The tango stops with a flourish right on BIG JOEY's "hey!" Finally giving up, ANNIE COOK gives a little scream and stomps off the stage. Turning around to see where the scream came from, PIERRE sees MUNCHOOS X. and JEALOUSY Y. for the first time, gasps, and turns white with horror. He moves his mouth to speak but, at first, nothing comes out.

PIERRE

J … J … J … Jealousy Y. Come Again? Speak of the devil but I was just telling Big Joey here what a fine mink stole them two dead Dalmation bitches of yours would have made on them incredible Come Again shoulders of yours …

PIERRE takes his remaining beer and stumbles backwards into the gambling "crowd."

BIG JOEY

So, Munchoos X. Luciano agreeable?

MUNCHOOS X. gives JEALOUSY Y. a thick wad of bills and sends her off to a "blackjack table."

MUNCHOOS X.

Go make yourself a little extra cash, princess. (*JEALOUSY leaves, MUNCHOOS sits, turns to BIG JOEY.*) Let's just say our meeting, in Toronto, went … well. Well?

BIG JOEY reaches into his jacket pocket and throws a sheaf of papers on the table.

BIG JOEY

Reads like a dream.

Taking his blessed time, MUNCHOOS takes his spectacles out of a pocket and leafs through the

*papers. Noticing that BIG JOEY is watching him with
a little too much hunger, MUNCHOOS stops, looks up,
glares at him.*

MUNCHOOS X.
 May I?

*Nervous as hell, though trying like the dickens not to
show it, BIG JOEY moves off. He goes to PIERRE and
whispers. On the little stage behind them, ANNIE
musters up the energy to go on with her song. Just as
she opens her mouth to sing, however, ROSABELLA
"bangs" the oom-chi-cha machine into action by
snapping into place, on her bum, a huge Las Vegas
showgirl's ostrich feather bustle. And again, the tango
begins, faintly at first, but then building and
building.*

BIG JOEY
 (*To PIERRE.*) I'm offering you a job, you toothless old
 bastard, Manager of Libations at Big Joey's Island of Gold
 Casino Royale. What the hell else do you want?

PIERRE
 A cut. On the livations. Seven percent. Or I ain't having
 nothing to do with no Come Again clan. Nope. Not one
 stitch of a gall darn thang. Tank you.

*JEALOUSY Y. appears right beside PIERRE. PIERRE tries
to bolt but BIG JOEY corners him. The two men begin
to circle each other, around the tall, statuesque,
Cruella-De-Vil-like JEALOUSY Y, as though they were
doing a tango.*

BIG JOEY
 Let me put it this way. I need one vote to get this casino
 resolution passed. And that one vote is yours.

PIERRE
 Then give me a cut on the privations.

*Pause. As the tango begins in earnest, up above,
ROSABELLA opens another bottle of wine.*

BIG JOEY
One percent.

PIERRE
Seven.

BIG JOEY
Two.

PIERRE
Seven.

BIG JOEY
Three.

PIERRE
Seven. Chikaboom.

BIG JOEY
Four. Chikaboom.

PIERRE
Seven.

BIG JOEY
Seven, I mean ...

PIERRE
Sold chikaboom chikaboom chikaboom, hey!

> *Up above, ROSABELLA finally pops open the bottle of wine, takes a slug, bangs the bottle down on the dresser, and does a stunning pose in the "mirror." The tango music comes to a spectacular finish right on PIERRE's "hey" with which PIERRE, in one spectacularly graceful tango move, throws BIG JOEY to the floor and disappears into the crowd. Ruffled mightily by the encounter, JEALOUSY Y. exits. And BIG JOEY, looking sheepish, looks over at MUNCHOOS X., who is just turning a page of the "budget" he has been studying all along. Upset to tears, ANNIE COOK hops off the stage and runs up to FRITZ.*

> *PIERRE pops back beside BIG JOEY.*

PIERRE

By the way ... (*Startled, BIG JOEY looks up.*) ... what the hell is a privations anyway?

BIG JOEY

"Libations." Means drinks. You're gonna be Manager of Bar Operations.

PIERRE

Holy shit la marde!

> *PIERRE pops out again. BIG JOEY plops himself down on the chair beside MUNCHOOS. PIERRE pops in again.*

PIERRE

I want that in writing.

> *BIG JOEY looks up. PIERRE stares him down. As BIG JOEY turns towards MUNCHOOS, PIERRE comes out with a tiny little:*

PIERRE

Chikaboom.

> *PIERRE disappears into the crowd as MUNCHOOS takes off his spectacles*

MUNCHOOS X.

Five hundred and fourteen grand. Hmph.

BIG JOEY

Don't think the Boccia brothers are gonna go for it? (*Pause. No answer.*) Too much?

MUNCHOOS X.

Not enough. Joe, we're talking big, me and the boys. I mean, way the hell bigger than this ...

BIG JOEY

Well, I been thinking of moving. To some place bigger.

MUNCHOOS X.

To where?

BIG JOEY

The Community Hall ... if the Band Council approves it ... but, then there's the Chief and her ... girls. Sure as hell can hold more than fifty people. Four hundred easy, I'd say. Say we get in there, make enough for a profit within, say, two, three years, build ourselves something brand new and then ...

MUNCHOOS X.

Joe, our friends down in Toronto, we're talking twenty point five million, for a brand new facility. And we're talking five, six months. So you go about your little community hall business, cuz I'm telling you, my mega palace is on its way and Wasy better be ready. Get it, Frilly Face?

A "slot machine" rings. Someone has just won a jackpot. FRITZ shows up at BIG JOEY's table, trailed by CREATURE and ANNIE.

FRITZ

Look here, Big Joey. You ask me to book my band in here for two weeks, 1 a.m. to 4 a.m., Thursday to Saturday. I ask for a union contract and you say there's none cuz this is Indian land and union rules don't apply, which is bullshit cuz the real reason is this place is not licensed to be serving alcohol much less allow gambling. Being the nice guy I am, I accept anyway. I get here, play my first coupla nights and what do I get?

Without warning, BIG JOEY backhands FRITZ, viciously, right across the face. FRITZ goes flying. BIG JOEY goes for him, picks him off the floor, raises him and throws him up against a "wall." Like a slab of meat, FRITZ collapses to the floor. Up above meanwhile, ROSABELLA shimmies into her showgirl ostrich feather headdress, almost ready now for her "show."

BIG JOEY

(*To FRITZ.*) Next time, I break both your arms.

The crowd suddenly parts, revealing EMILY, LIZ and PUSSY standing in the middle of the room. Stunning in black leather, they are looking at BIG JOEY with ice cool eyes.

CREATURE

Ho-leeee! Emily Dictionary! Big Joey, it's Emily
Dictionary! Come to throw another one of them deadly
curses on you like she did last time she was here five years
ago, remember, Big Joey, when she was pregnant with
that baby she said was yours and then Gazelle Nataways ...

*FRITZ uses the opportunity to stagger away while
ANNIE scurries over towards EMILY. As BIG JOEY,
meanwhile, struts over towards them, EMILY keeps her
eyes glued to his.*

EMILY

(*Ice cold.*) Joe.

*But PUSSY goes weak at the knees at the sight of the
impossibly handsome, and very studly, BIG JOEY.*

PUSSY

Oh, my stars.

BIG JOEY

So, Emily. You come to tell me you still want my dick?

EMILY

Big Joey? Meet a coupla buddies of mine, come all the
way from California just to see your Juke Joint.

PUSSY

(*Playing up to BIG JOEY.*) This is it? I heard it was much ...
bigger. (*Laughs affectedly.*)

BIG JOEY

(*To LIZ, immediately drawn by her stunning looks.*) Oh, it gets
bigger as the night gets longer ... (*Reaching for LIZ's hand,
intending to kiss it.*) ... know what I mean?

LIZ

(*Turning kiss into a firm handshake.*) Yeah, I know what you
mean. I work in a slaughter house and after a while, meat
becomes, well, just ... meat. (*Beat.*) Liz Jones. Dyke.

*LIZ raises BIG JOEY's hand, intending to kiss it. BIG
JOEY pulls his hand away, repulsed. EMILY grabs
FRITZ by the scruff of the neck, lifts him, carries him
and plunks him down on the little "stage."*

EMILY

> (*To FRITZ.*) E minor, A minor, B seven, A minor, back to E
> minor.

>> *As EMILY chats up the band, getting them ready for
>> performance and as LIZ helps her get things together
>> on stage, PUSSY catches sight of the motorcycle at rest
>> against the wall. On her way to the stage, she stops
>> and touches it, knowing full well that BIG JOEY's eyes
>> are glued to her.*

BIG JOEY

> So. You're one of them legendary biker mamas Emily was
> telling me about. You still ride?

PUSSY

> Uh-uh. We quit. All of us.

BIG JOEY

> Emily, too, huh? (*PUSSY nods.*) Funny the way she freaks
> out every time she sees one of them things. Something
> happened, huh? (*Pause.*)

PUSSY

> (*Caressing the bike, lovingly.*) Harley.

BIG JOEY

> Buddy of mine, Black Eye Kananakeesik, played one
> game of craps too many the other night.

PUSSY

> Can I touch it? Can I squeeze it?

BIG JOEY

> You wouldn't wanna go for a little ride on it, would ya?
> Later on tonight?

PUSSY

> Maybe? But aren't you already ... with ... someone?

BIG JOEY

> (*His mouth closer and closer to hers.*) I'll ... send her
> shopping. Sudbury. She *loves* shopping.

>> *He reaches for a kiss. PUSSY pulls away at the last
>> second and climbs on to the little "stage." The
>> moment PUSSY starts singing, BIG JOEY stands rooted,*

awed by her beauty, her charisma. High up above,
ROSABELLA slides into elbow-length opera gloves and
her shocking-red stilettos, then stands there grooving
to the song.

EMILY/LIZ/PUSSY
(*Singing.*) "She used to chuckle,
She used to laugh and bubble,
Cuz she took a fascination
In her life and all its trouble;
Took the heartache and the sorrow,
Put 'em in her pocket and she
Jumbled all the rain and clouds and sunshine,
Boom-dee-boom chika-chee cha-la-la chicka-chee;
She used to par-tay,
She used to pose and sashay
As she'd take her life and lovin'
In her hand and fling them away;
Took the chills and spills and horrors,
Put 'em in her pocket and she
Jumbled all the rage and pain and laughter,
Boom-dee-boom chika-chee cha-la-la chika-chee.

Oh, she was a doll,
Oh, she was the one, woe-woe."

> *During the instrumental break, GAZELLE NATAWAYS*
> *sashays in, now all dolled up. Terrified that she and*
> *EMILY are going to kill each other, CREATURE scurries*
> *out. Shocked to see EMILY there, GAZELLE locks eyes*
> *with her: the encounter is ferocious. Her face burning*
> *with hatred, EMILY finally manages to pull her gaze*
> *away. Somewhat discombobulated, GAZELLE turns her*
> *attention to BIG JOEY. Seeing him entranced by PUSSY,*
> *she sashays up to him, femme fatale to the hilt.*

GAZELLE
Jealousy Y. Come Again was telling me the best stores on
Rodeo Drive get their summer collection in as early as
March. (*No response from BIG JOEY.*) Pooch? (*Still no*
response. Louder.) I said, Jealousy Y. Come Again says the

best stores on Rodeo Drive get their summer collection in as early as March.

Seeing that not only is her man being bewitched by PUSSY COMMANDA but that MS. COMMANDA is playing him for all he's worth, GAZELLE sashays out the door, fuming with outrage.

EMILY/LIZ/PUSSY
(*Singing.*) "She used to chuckle,
She used to laugh and bubble,
Cuz she took a fascination
In her life and all its trouble;
Took the heartache and the sorrow,
Put 'em in her pocket and she
Jumbled all the rain and clouds and sunshine,
Boom-dee-boom chika-chee cha-la-la chicka-chee;
She used to par-tay,
She used to pose and sashay
As she'd take her life and lovin'
In her hand and fling them away;
Took the chills and spills and horrors,
Put 'em in her pocket and she
Jumbled all the rage and pain and laughter,
Boom-dee-boom chika-chee cha-la-la chika-chee.

Oh, she was a doll,
Oh, she was the one, woe-woe ... " (*Repeat, as needed.*)

Fade-out. The Juke Joint is going to rock tonight!

Scene Six: Community Hall

In the dimness, an Indian chief headdress descends slowly from the ceiling. When the lights come up, we are at the Community Hall where CHIEF BIG ROSE sits humming to herself as she works on this headdress, now landed right in her hands. Suddenly, the "door" flies open and VERONIQUE ST. PIERRE comes charging in.

CHIEF BIG ROSE
Lock that door!

VERONIQUE
(*Stops. Whispers.*) Are we being watched?

CHIEF BIG ROSE
Yes, Veronique St. Pierre, we are being watched.

*VERONIQUE locks the "door," turns and zooms across
the room to sit with CHIEF BIG ROSE.*

VERONIQUE
(*Loud.*) I just narrowly escaped being battered to death
right on top of your dead brother's grave at the extreme
western edge of the Wasaychigan Hill cemetery ...

CHIEF BIG ROSE
... an excellent place to die ...

VERONIQUE
... as I was reciting my rosaries and wailing away with the
most powerful hymns in my repertoire right there at the
grave of your dead brother Morty Moosetail who the
people on this reserve constantly seem to forget was my
first and favourite husband, may he rest in peace, when
guess whose head slithers out from among the
tombstones but my second husband Pierre St. Pierre, I
just about had a heart attack, whereupon he flung
himself upon my person and accused me of spending too
much time at his rival's grave at which point that poor
simple wooden crucifix on your dead brother's grave fell
over with a thud and made Pierre St. Pierre confess that
Big Joey and Munchoos X Come Again are planning to
approach the Mafia in Sudbury for help with their
expansion of Big Joey's casino.

CHIEF BIG ROSE
I didn't know they had the Mafia in Sudbury.

VERONIQUE
That's what I told Pierre St. Pierre.

CHIEF BIG ROSE

And Jealousy Y. Come Again is taking Italian lessons, someone was telling me. Hmmm, methinks I begin to see a certain pattern here.

GAZELLE

(*Off-stage.*) Aieee! (*VERONIQUE rushes to a "window."*) What are you trying to do, kill me? Get some men out here, I don't trust you Moose triplets.

VERONIQUE

Goooooood! That pig Big Joey finally had the sense to beat the living daylights out of that slut Gazelle Nataways ... (*Gasps, thrilled to near tears.*) ... the triplets Marjorie Moose, Maggie May Moose and Mighty Moose just dropped Gazelle Nataways on the front steps of the health clinic. (*Reels back to her seat.*)

CHIEF BIG ROSE

Now listen to me, Veronique St. Pierre. I want you to tell your husband not to take Big Joey's offer of a job as Manager of Salvation, or some such thing, or he will regret it. Bribing Band Councillors is a criminal act, as a woman of your stature must surely know. Tell him to use that last crucial vote against this horrible casino business to help us, help me, help the people of this reserve. Please?

VERONIQUE

I have a weak heart, you know?

During the next speech, a dim light comes up to reveal CREATURE NATAWAYS, skulking just outside a "window," surreptitiously audio-taping CHIEF BIG ROSE.

CHIEF BIG ROSE

If you do this, not only will I help you find a new doctor for your weak heart, not only will I help you find a new stove for your roast beef à la chipoocheech, but I personally will see to it that Veronique St. Pierre will be at the front of the motorcade that escorts me to the signing

of the first Indian treaty in a hundred years. With
Premier Bob.

*Finished "taping," CREATURE skulks off. Light out on
him. In the Community Hall, meanwhile,
VERONIQUE, for once, sits speechless, near tears.
Rising, CHIEF BIG ROSE brings the partly finished
headdress to her.*

Now I want you to model this for me.

*CHIEF BIG ROSE puts the headdress on VERONIQUE's
head and scrutinizes it. VERONIQUE looks absolutely
ridiculous.*

Rose pink. My official colour ...

Fade-out.

Scene Seven: Emily's Living Room, The Black Cat Soirée, Emily's Front Yard

Song(s): "She Was a Doll" and "Jukebox Lady"

*At Emily's, FRITZ, having set up a makeshift
"recording studio" in Emily's living room, sits at a
"control panel" keeping watch over sound levels,
running over once to reposition a mike at EMILY's
mouth, etc. EMILY, PUSSY and LIZ are wearing
headphones, listening to the playback on their vocals
for "She Was a Doll." ANNIE grooves in the
background.*

EMILY/LIZ/PUSSY
    (*Singing.*) "She used to par-tay,
    She used to pose and sashay
    As she'd take her life and lovin'
    In her hand and fling them away;
    Took the chills and spills and horrors,
    Put 'em in her pocket and she
    Jumbled all the rage and pain and laughter,
    Boom-dee-boom chika-chee cha-la-la chika-chee.

Oh, she was a doll,
Oh, she was the one, woe-woe."

> *FRITZ flicks the machinery on to play back the song
> just recorded. The song plays in the background,
> EMILY, LIZ and PUSSY singing and humming along
> quietly during parts of FRITZ's next two speeches.*

FRITZ

You girls, you girls, you are gur-rate! The way you do that
boom-dee-boom chika-chee cha-la-la-wha! With a band
like mine backing you up we could be doing the Queen
of Hearts in North Bay, the Whitewater Inn in
Kapuskasing, you name it, heck, give me three months
and I can get us a gig at the El Mocambo in Toronto,
upstairs! But we'll need a name. I mean, we really oughta
slap a name on this demo-tape like, right tonight, like,
something snazzy, something sexy, something that'll stick
to the ribs, like ...

LIZ

(*Uninterested, sarcastic.*) Squaws for Jesus.

FRITZ

Well, something with a Native flavour like, like ... the
Dream Visionettes, the Pow Wowettes, the Aboriginelles,
or, or, or something with an animal twist like ... (*Suddenly
wary of LIZ.*) And you ... are saying, correct me if I'm
wrong, you ... are saying you wrote, actually wrote ...
these songs?

PUSSY

Are you suggesting she stole them?

FRITZ

Anything's possible. The biz, law suits, a man's gotta
know where he stands, I mean, who's gonna believe that
an Indian girl ...

LIZ

Look, Mr. Katz. I may be just a full-blooded cute little
Sioux Indian woman from the Rosebud Indian
Reservation to you but I also happen to be a graduate of
the North Dakota Conservatory of Music. I know my

harmony, I know my sonata form, I can tell you the difference between a spicatto, pizzicato, ostinato, cold tomato, hot spaghetti, you name it. The Fargo Philharmonic may not be the Berlin Philharmonic but you are looking at the very first Native person, in history, male or female, to conduct a symphony orchestra.

PUSSY

You conducted the Fargo Philharmonic? You never told me that.

LIZ

(*To PUSSY.*) I never talk about it. (*To FRITZ.*) So, take us, you furry little white dude, what the hell, you only live once, take us to the El Mocambo.

FRITZ

But ya *got* to have a name.

PUSSY

Crème de la crème.

EMILY

(*Hard.*) No.

FRITZ

Not bad. A little long-winded.

PUSSY

Rose'd love it. (*To ANNIE.*) She used to call Emily that. We'd be riding down the freeway and Rose's voice would boom out on the CB. "Emily Dictionary, you old dyke you, you are the crème de la crème of my life."

EMILY

I said no! (*A knock. She yells at the "door."*) Yes?

FRITZ

That's it, that's it. I see it. Frederick Stephen Katz ... Productions ... Presents ... "The LaCreams!"

LIZ

(*Dismissive.*) Pfff.

> *The motorcycle from Big Joey's stands at the open "door," a big pink bow on the handle bar, a huge*

bouquet of roses sits on the seat, with two gift-
wrapped boxes. CREATURE wheels it in.

CREATURE

Special delivery. From Joseph Jeremiah McLeod.

EMILY

What the hell do you think you're doing?

CREATURE

Says right here: "Deliver right into her living room."

EMILY

Get that thing outta here. Creature Nataways. Get that
fucking thing right outta here.

CREATURE

I tole you once, I tole you twice, Emily Dictionary, I'm
only the delivery man. (*Takes off.*)

PUSSY takes the presents, reads the card attached and
rips open her present, a pink negligee, obviously
Gazelle's.

PUSSY

Oh, my stars.

LIZ unwraps her present, a huge dildo, and reads the
card attached, silently. PUSSY moves over to read over
her shoulder.

PUSSY

(*Reading aloud.*) "Welcome to Wasy, Ms. Jones. All a
woman like you needs is one good night in the arms of a
real man. Have a good practice. With this." The nerve.

LIZ tosses the dildo aside.

EMILY

Fritz, roll this thing outta here.

FRITZ and ANNIE wheel the bike off with difficulty.
PUSSY takes a deep breath, then, like a swimmer
coming up for air:

PUSSY

I'm going over. (*Beat.*) To his place.

EMILY

The hell for?

PUSSY

(*Blushing.*) To ... to thank him. What else?

EMILY

Are you crazy?

PUSSY

(*Finding a foothold.*) Hey. We're supposed to be spies, remember? For a certain woman chief? Well, where better to do it from than ... you know. (*Begins to leave.*)

LIZ

(*Yelling.*) Puss!

> EMILY *rushes forward to grab* PUSSY, *who whips around, livid.*

PUSSY

Look. You're the ones always talking about how we gotta stop them stomping all over us women. Look at you now. All talk, no action. Remember Rose? Remember what she did to that asshole that one night? Slid into them flaming red six inch stilettos of hers, cleavage to the navel, enticed him into her confidence, primed him like a pump, and then, arghh, sunk her teeth into his tongue, dragged him to the door, down that fire escape and spat him out into the street. "Pah! Last fucking time that one's gonna give a woman any more of that male shit," she said. Remember? (*Leaves.*) See ya in a bit.

LIZ

(*Bitter.*) Bruised, battered and bloodied.

EMILY

Then go with her.

LIZ

What good would that do? She doesn't listen to me. She never listens to me. Okay, okay, my hands are clean. Ain't having no more to do with it. I don't give a good god damn. It happens every time, Emily. I tell her: "Puss, you're doing it again," but you can't stop her. Rose herself used to tell her the same thing, over and over and over …

At the top of heap of "motorcycles" (and motorcycle parts, mostly handlebars), the "jukebox" appears (though not yet "alive," not yet lit up). And the drunken ghost of ROSABELLA JEAN BAEZ, all decked out as showgirl—looking like some legendary bird of paradise, spectacular—staggers towards it.

EMILY

He's gonna kill her. Maybe not today …

EMILY/ROSABELLA

… maybe not physically, but he's gonna kill her …

EMILY turns slowly to look up at ROSABELLA, hardly aware any longer of LIZ. Away off in the background, the women at the Black Cat Soirée move on and form a frozen tableau, dark, moody and funky/romantic.

LIZ

Wednesday, the third of July, 1985. The Black Cat Soirée, 296 Mission Street, San Francisco, California. You, me, Pussy Commanda, Hortensia Colorado, Rosabella Jean Baez and seventeen other women, twenty-one in total, twenty-one fabulous Indian women on Harleys, we take off, it's midnight and by two a.m., we're travelling south on the coast highway, Rose at the head …

ROSABELLA throws a hand across the jukebox to steady herself. The jukebox flickers to life, its lights heartbreaking. And it plays, softly at first, "Honky Tonk Angels" by Kitty Wells. The women at the Black Cat Soirée begin moving sensually in time to the music.

… you and Pussy Commanda on each side of her, the rest of us in V-formation behind you. Rose, when she was still alive, and she'd say: "we women got no power. We ain't never gonna get no power/ …

ROSABELLA

(*Drunkenly.*) ... /ain't never gonna get no power. Tell me.
When's it gonna change, huh, when's it all gonna
change?"

LIZ

Remember those words, Em? Rose's words? That was the
last night of her life. Emily, we want you to come down to
San Francisco, with us. That's why we came here. The Rez
Sisters, they sent us. We, all of us, we're gonna do a
memorial ride to Rose. Emily. (*No response.*) Emily?

As LIZ fades into the shadows like a dream,
ROSABELLA caresses the jukebox.

ROSABELLA

I remember the day the first jukebox arrived in Reindeer
Lake. Mrs. Permachuk, this little old Russian woman, first
white woman ever to come north and trade furs with the
Indians. She brought this jukebox with her, put it in her
store, first one ever seen up there. She'd sit there beside
it, day after day, just a-wailing along to all them country
songs. Somewhere behind that glass, women sang away
their love and all their pain. (*Lovingly, respectfully.*) Kitty
Wells, Kitty Wells ... (*Wails an ear-piercing, insane "lu-lu-
lu."*) ... lu-lu-lu-lu-lu-lu-lu-lu-lu ever wondered what the
mountains of Nepal must look like? In the rain? Or the
pampas of Argentina, the beaches of Rio?

EMILY

(*Softly, tenderly, as if to herself.*) Yes.

ROSABELLA

Let's escape, let's fly, you and me, to some place where
no one can hurt us. Have you ever wondered what the
other side must look like, Emily, how beautiful it must be?
Soft, pink-coloured light all around you, sweet, sweet
music washing over your skin, all your worries, all your
aches and pains, all ... all gone ...

EMILY

(*Roars a vitriolic, hateful roar.*) Ohhhhh, I hate it, hate it,
just fucking hate it when you talk like that!

EMILY flicks her lit cigarette, hatefully, straight at
ROSABELLA and walks out. ROSE brushes the cigarette
off, throws one of her red stilettos at EMILY and
screams.

ROSABELLA

Ya fucking bitch! Yeah! Ride that beast. Cuz you know
what? That's the only way you're ever gonna be able to
get away from me and when you do, the only place
you'll end up in is right here in my arms, ma crème de
la crème ...

The introduction to "Jukebox Lady" begins, softly,
slowly, getting ever louder, as EMILY slowly walks
back into her living room, livid.

ROSABELLA

... arms just a-waiting for ya filled with roses, heart just a-
waiting for ya filled with roses, I have no blood left in my
veins, Emily, not one drop, veins are filled, filled with
roses, roses, roses ... (*Laughs insanely.*)

Not taking a breath, ROSE begins singing as, at the
same time, she begins moving away from the jukebox
and down to Emily's living room.

ROSABELLA

(*Singing.*) "She is the Jukebox Lady,
She dances through the light
Of pale, pink-coloured glass,
Her eyes white flames in the night;
Hey there, Ojibway lady,
Your time's not here it seems;
Those far away tomorrows
Remain but soft-coloured dreams.

How long since you became
A victim of such rage;
And how much longer will you
Remain in your glass cage?
Hey there, Ojibway lady,
Your time's not here it seems;

Those far away tomorrows,
Remain but soft-coloured dreams."

> *By the instrumental break, ROSE is dancing with
> EMILY, a slow, beautiful "last call" waltz, at the San
> Francisco Club called The Black Cat Soirée. Then
> ROSE wends her drunken way to the top of the trash
> heap where a motorcycle appears standing behind the
> coloured glass of the "jukebox"—a dream illusion.
> Slowly, drunkenly, ROSE straddles the bike.*

EMILY

(*Shrieking.*) No! No! Never again! Never again! Never,
never, never, never ... (*Singing, eyes streaming*)
"How long since you became
A victim of such rage;
And how much longer will you
Remain in your glass cage?"

> *ROSE kick-starts her bike and revs it up as EMILY
> continues singing.*

EMILY

(*Singing.*) "Hey there, Ojibway lady,
Your time's not here it seems;
Those far away tomorrows,
Remain but soft-coloured dreams."

> *Through this visual, as the instrumental break from
> the song returns once more, the sound of an
> approaching transport truck surfaces from under it,
> it's horn honking intermittently, it's headlights,
> particularly on ROSABELLA, growing in intensity.*
>
> *The music hits a deafening silence. The transport
> truck "rams" into ROSABELLA's motorcycle. There is a
> blinding flash of light, women scream, and
> ROSABELLA grips her heart, letting it go with a snap.
> A shower of American beauty pink rose petals explodes
> from the heart as the heart itself slowly "rises" up to
> the night sky, gently "knocks" the round full moon
> out of the way, and becomes a gorgeous heart-shaped
> pink moon in its place as ...*

*American beauty pink rose petals come floating, like
snow, from the rafters as, under them, BIG JOEY
carries a naked PUSSY COMMANDA to a bed of pink
roses, lays her down gently on it, and then scatters
rose petals over her, bathing her as ... A black-eyed,
broken-armed GAZELLE NATAWAYS looks bitterly on,
and, from a distance, LIZ JONES watches PUSSY sadly
and EMILY watches in disgust.*

*Fade-out, as the instrumental from "Jukebox Lady"
billows out into a huge, heartbreaking crescendo.
And begins fading into silence as ... In her "yard,"
EMILY straddles her bike, the bike facing the audience.
She kick starts it. It gives off a deafening rev. And
EMILY DICTIONARY "rides" her motorcycle as ...*

*In the night sky, only ROSABELLA's heart—the full
moon, pink, gorgeous—remains visible. Fade-out.
And, in the final silence (and darkness): the sound
of a human heart beating.*

ACT TWO

Scene Eight: The Hilarium, Big Joey's Basement, The Hilarium

Song(s): "The Hilarium" and "Keespin Kisagee-in"

A pin spot snaps on, revealing ROSABELLA JEAN BAEZ, showgirl from hell, standing leaning with a hand on her "jukebox." With a flourish of her other hand, she makes her moon/heart appear in the night sky, from there to shine a soft pink light on the village of Wasy far below. Then with a throaty laugh, she blows a kiss at the audience. And fades into the darkness.

At Chief Big Rose's, the CHIEF stands conferring (wordlessly) with GAZELLE, the latter with a black eye and one arm in a cast. EMILY enters. All too aware of the hate that exists between the two, the CHIEF moves in—come what may, as Chief "of the people," she will "cancel" this hate.

CHIEF BIG ROSE
Ahem. Ladies? I thank you for coming. Now, while we wait for the other two ... ladies, watch.

With a grin, she turns to a tall avocado plant that droops in a pot on a stand between GAZELLE and EMILY. With wizard-like gestures, she tries levitating the stem of the plant, to no avail.

CHIEF BIG ROSE
    Rise. I command you to rise!

    *She yanks the stem to a standing position. In a flash
    of pink that lights up the night sky, ROSABELLA snaps
    her fingers, making ROSETTA DICTIONARY (a ghost
    girl of five) "pop" out of nowhere. Silently, ROSETTA
    "makes" the plant droop again.*

    (*Wounded.*) Ohhhh. (*Looks, with despair, at her "glass
    walls."*) It's my son down in Toronto, picking up them
    whitemanish, "oh, excusez moi" sorta ways. You know
    what they call this kind of room down there? A solarium.
    Tom tells me it makes vegetation flourish and the human
    mind expand but all it's done is kill every seed I've
    planted. You have no idea how many avocado plants have
    died in this ... solarium ... and gone to avocado heaven,
    there to dance their little avocado hearts to eternity. So
    you know what I'm doing? With this room? I'm
    cancelling the solarium and turning it into: a hilarium!

EMILY
    A hilarium?

GAZELLE
    What the hell's a hilarium?

    *Stuffed monkey stuck to back, tiny hurdy-gurdy in
    hand, ROSETTA appears above the women and plays
    jolly, hippity-hoppity music. So charmed by the
    CHIEF's ridiculous behaviour are GAZELLE and EMILY
    they soon forget the tension between them, at least for
    the moment. By song's end, the place is exploding
    with a manic, "toontown" energy.*

CHIEF BIG ROSE
    (*Speaks/sings.*) You see, my dears, as Chief of the People,
    The way I see it is this:
    The world takes itself too seriously,
    Too seriously, way too serious;
    Biz-ness, for instance, the world of politics,
    Law, religion, you name it, it's always
    Men who run these things, ain't that too bad?

EMILY/GAZELLE
It's too sad for words.

CHIEF BIG ROSE
Hitler, for instance, or Stalin, Pol Pot or
Vlad the Impaler, Idi Amin or that
Rat Mussolini, any idea, had they
Speckle or smidgen of any idea of
Laughter, merriment, jollity, mirth, did they
Know how to laugh or chuckle or giggle,
Hee-hee, ha-ha, ho-ho?

EMILY/GAZELLE
Hell, no!

CHIEF BIG ROSE
This Premier Bob, for instance, if flabby-cheeked,
Serious Premier Bob were to come here to
Wasy, we'd sign the treaty, I'd shake his
Hand, I'd give him his headdress then bring him in
Here and tickle him here and tickle him
There and jiggle him here and jiggle him there.

EMILY/GAZELLE
Oh, chick-a dee-doo, chick-a-dee-dee.

CHIEF BIG ROSE
Until he's laughing with animal gusto,
He's bent over double and inches from death;
Politicians, hmph! That's what they
Need is a chamber to chuckle, a chamber to
Chortle, a chamber to giggle, a chamber to
Jiggle and laugh.

EMILY
A hilarium? Well, tickle my titties,

GAZELLE
Well, tickle mine, too.

CHIEF BIG ROSE
Ha!

> *Instrumental/dance break. Seven avocado plants
> come dancing on in classic Ukrainian-Cossack*

*kick-line fashion and proceed to put on a show from
hell—or rather from heaven for that's who they are,
all those avocado plants who've died and gone to
avocado heaven "there to dance their little avocado
hearts to eternity," as CHIEF BIG ROSE imagines, and
describes, them. At one point—and just as LIZ and
PUSSY enter and stand there watching amazed—the
plants grab EMILY and GAZELLE and dance with
them, in the middle of which, EMILY screams:*

EMILY
(*Shreiking with glee.*) I can't believe it! I'm dancing with an
avocado plant!

> *Instrumental/dance break over, CHIEF BIG ROSE
> resumes her song.*

CHIEF BIG ROSE
Except that Premier Bob ...

EMILY
Premier Bob Rae?

CHIEF BIG ROSE
I've cancelled him ...

GAZELLE
You've cancelled him?

CHIEF BIG ROSE
Yes!

EMILY/GAZELLE
Oh!

CHIEF BIG ROSE
Brian Mulroney is coming instead.

LIZ
Brian Mulroney?

PUSSY
Who's Brian Mulroney?

EMILY
(*To LIZ and PUSSY.*) He's our Prime Minister.

GAZELLE

(*To LIZ and PUSSY, joking/taunting.*) Yanks!

CHIEF BIG ROSE

He has Indian blood, so he whispered to me,
By phone, of course, so I whispered to him,
"Give us the island."

EMILY

Manitoulin?

CHIEF BIG ROSE

Right! And he said, "yes," so he's coming instead,
We'll sign the treaty, I'll shake his hand,
Give him his headdress, then bring him in
Here and tickle him here and tickle him
There and jiggle him here and jiggle him there …

EMILY/GAZELLE/LIZ/PUSSY

Oh, chick-a dee-doo, chick-a dee-dee!

CHIEF BIG ROSE

Until he's laughing with animal gusto,
He's bent over double and inches from death
Politicians, hmph! That's what they
Need is a chamber to chuckle, a chamber to
Chortle, a chamber to giggle, a chamber to
Jiggle and laugh.

ALL

A chamber to chuckle, a chamber to chortle,
A chamber to giggle, a chamber to jiggle and laugh, ha!

*During the last part of the song, the avocado plants
have gone dancing gently off, like the chorus-line of
cartoon characters at the end of the "Bugs Bunny
Show." When all are gone and silence returns, CHIEF
BIG ROSE, EMILY, GAZELLE, LIZ and PUSSY stand
panting. Until stark reality seeps back in.*

GAZELLE

Well, irrigate my ovaries, but if it ain't Ms. Pussy
Comman*ding* herself.

CHIEF BIG ROSE

Now, I will have no fighting in here, do you hear me?
This is a hilarium, not a fight-a-tarium.

GAZELLE

(*Scintillating, to* PUSSY.) You like my *awn-sawm-bla?* The
white stone glove, the eye shadow, the little islands of
crimson splashed hither and yon across my fair bazoom?
It ain't Estee Lauder, I'll tell you *that* much, Ms.
Comman*ding.*

For a second, PUSSY *may well jump* GAZELLE *but for*
EMILY *and* LIZ *taking one step forward to block her*
way.

It's all natural colouring, all come from right here on the
Rez, wanna see more? You wanna see the tiger stripes on
my back? The purple bruisettes up and down my
voluptuous thighs, my sensuous behind, my immaculate
… immaculata? Man-made, Ms. Comman*ding,* every one
of 'em and you, too, can get 'em, cuz they're available
right there in my bed of roses which, I understand,
you've recently inherited, no? (*Long, dangerous silence.*)

CHIEF BIG ROSE

Ahem. Women? Now I called you here to … to rally our
forces against that rat, Big Joey, and this casino … pipe-
dream of his.

Aware that EMILY, LIZ *and* PUSSY *are looking at*
GAZELLE *with daggers, the* CHIEF *goads* GAZELLE.

Ms … Nataways? Your story, please?

GAZELLE

(*Crushing avocado bulb in hand.*) Yessss, babe, oooh yessss.
(*To women.*) That's what I'm doing to Joe first chance I
get.

CHIEF BIG ROSE

Meaning?

EMILY

> (*Still distrustful.*) Oh, I get it. She's on our side now, is
> she? (*The CHIEF nods. Pause.*) Okay? Sister Rose? It's your
> funeral.
>
>> *Beat. Ever the level-headed stateswoman, the CHIEF*
>> *goes on to the next item on her "agenda."*

CHIEF BIG ROSE

> (*To LIZ and PUSSY.*) Well? Spies? Your most recent ...
> research? If you please?

PUSSY

> (*Swallowing her fear of GAZELLE.*) Vice-Chief Come Again is
> plotting your impeachment.

CHIEF BIG ROSE

> (*Disgusted.*) That Munchoos X. will go to any length to
> get his old job back, won't he? Well, I'm sorry, but I'm
> hanging on to this Chiefdom until the people vote me
> away.

PUSSY

> But Jealousy Y. says Munchoos X. has a tape that proves
> you've been trying to buy Pierre St. Pierre's vote for your
> side of the casino debate by baiting his wife with you
> kitchen stoves, a place in your motorcade ...
> (*Disbelieving.*) ... a heart transplant?

CHIEF BIG ROSE

> (*Blushing.*) Then you, as my spies, *must* get that ...
>
>> *Pause. Away up in the night sky, the showgirl*
>> *ROSABELLA fleetingly appears, sending down a*
>> *"spell" with the gesture of a hand. In the hilarium, a*
>> *"darkness" falls, as if a cloud has suddenly diffused*
>> *the light of the sun, or a shadow, perhaps even a*
>> *ghost, has entered the room. And everyone there can*
>> *feel it.*
>
> (*Spooked.*) ... tape. (*Likewise spooked, everyone remains*
> *frozen.*) Darn, I'm gonna have to tell Philomena to alter
> the size of that headdress. They say Brian Mulroney's
> head is twice the size of Premier Bob's. (*Exits.*)

PUSSY

Oh, Christ. Look at the time. Joe ... (*Stops herself, shoots GAZELLE a scared little glance, then goes on.*) ... he'll ... be home any minute and he ... doesn't like it when I'm not ... not there.

GAZELLE

(*Dangerous.*) Ciao, bella. (*PUSSY leaves. Silence.*) Ow, my arm ...

LIZ

Emily?

Finding EMILY rooted, as if trapped by GAZELLE's eyes, LIZ waits for a response from her, gets none and, after a moment's uncertainty, leaves as well.

"Sent" by ROSABELLA, ROSETTA DICTIONARY "pops" out of a "wall" and, dressed as a miniature Hallowe'en witch, a broom over her shoulder like a shovel, she marches figure eights around EMILY and GAZELLE, who stand there staring at each other (and, of course, unseeing of the "ghost," ROSETTA).

ROSETTA

Mama. Mama. Pagitinin tanee-taweegeeyan. Eewa? Pagitinin tanee-taweegeeyan. (Mommy. Mommy. Let me be born. Please? Let me be born.) (*Repeat as needed.*)

From the surrounding darkness, ROSABELLA's throaty laugh resounds, echoed by ROSETTA's little giggle (interspersed with the English translation to her words). The giggle, in particular, echoes and re-echoes, like a breeze at play—as if, suddenly, the room is filled with the giggles of "little spirit girls," that is, little girls not yet born.

EMILY

(*Terrified.*) She's ... she's here. My baby ...

GAZELLE

Don't be silly ...

EMILY

(*Looking desperately around.*) Rosetta?

70

GAZELLE

(*Now spooked too.*) Who are you talking ... Em. Your sister, the Chief, she brought us here to talk. Now let's ...

ROSABELLA's and ROSETTA's laughter/giggles resonate, "inside" EMILY's mind.

EMILY

St ... st ... stop ... stop it! Rosetta? Don't do this to me. Please? Rosetta? You are dead, you are dead, you were *not* born, you were ...

In his basement Juke Joint, BIG JOEY stands admiring his studly reflection in a "mirror."

GAZELLE

It was ... it was ... Joe made me do it.

EMILY

Yeah, blame him. As if he willed your foot to kick *his* baby outta my gut.

GAZELLE

He was mine. Joe was mine. You had no right to come between us like ... (*EMILY coming at her, GAZELLE backs away.*) ... like that.

EMILY

You jealous, self-centred, heartless ... you kicked my belly. You killed my Rosetta, killed her in my belly five years ago.

BIG JOEY fades away. And now, it is as if EMILY and GAZELLE are caught in a time warp. The lullaby from the song, "When Children Sleep," snaps, huge, symphonic, as EMILY and GAZELLE re-live ROSETTA's death, EMILY screaming, falling to the ground, GAZELLE kicking her belly, over and over. All while ROSETTA runs around EMILY and GAZELLE, screaming at them—ROSABELLA watching her from above, as if guiding her.

ROSETTA

Mama. Mama. Pagitinin tanee-taweegeeyan. Eewa?
Pagitinin tanee-taweegeeyan. (Mommy. Mommy. Let me
be born. Please? Let me be born.) (*Repeat as needed.*)

*Laughing and crying, the voices of infants-never-
born fill the theatre. And, in heartbreaking slow
motion, EMILY gives birth, ROSETTA crawling out
from between her thighs, EMILY screaming with agony,
GAZELLE with horror, as she, GAZELLE, tries
desperately to blot out the sight.*

GAZELLE

No! No! No! No! No! No! No!

ROSETTA standing again, she sings lovingly to EMILY.

ROSETTA

Keespin kisagee-in, seemak kaweecheewin ... (If you love
me, you will come with me ...)

*The lullaby from "When Children Sleep" and the little
girl voices snap off just as EMILY grabs GAZELLE by
the throat. GAZELLE bangs EMILY's head with the cast
on her arm. Both howl with pain.*

*ROSETTA angrily "levitates" the avocado pot and
"commands" it to dump soil and dead plant all over
the two women who have now wrestled themselves to
the floor, grunting and groaning. Startled, they look
up at the "floating" pot and scramble from beneath it.
ROSETTA drops the pot; it crashes to the floor. Spooked,
the women scream. "Directed" by ROSABELLA from
above, ROSETTA tickles EMILY, then GAZELLE, until
both are in stitches, holding on to each other like
sisters. Having hit rock bottom in her grief, EMILY has
survived, is now capable of unbelievable human
feats, including forgiving her most hated enemy,
GAZELLE.*

*Proud of her handiwork, ROSETTA marches off, broom
over shoulder, right through a "wall." From above,
ROSABELLA throws EMILY a great big kiss. And
disappears.*

CHIEF BIG ROSE, wondering what the hell is going on, pops her head in. When she sees these two women—of all people—holding each other jiggling with hysteria, she smiles broadly.

CHIEF BIG ROSE
(*To audience.*) See? It works. My hilarium works.

Brief instrumental reprise of "The Hilarium." And blackout.

Scene Nine: The Community Hall

At the Community Hall, HERA is only half done Bob Rae's black-and-white Indian chief headdress while PHILOMENA is almost finished Chief Big Rose's pink one.

HERA
You know, you really should try it on her head before you alter its size again. If I can get Premier Bob's head measurements faxed to me from Toronto, surely you can …

PHILOMENA
Ha! Try getting Pelajia Rosella Patchnose—Chief Big Rose to the world!—to sit still long enough to have her head measured. You know, Hera Keechigeesik, I think I am going to ask Veronique St. Pierre and her husband to go and steal that wooden Indian chief from the Come Again mansion.

HERA
Hmmm-mmm?

PHILOMENA
So that, at least, some semblawnce … (*i.e. French pronunciation of the word, "semblance."*) … of an Indian chief can model this headdress for me from time to time as it nears the finish.

The "phone" rings. HERA picks it up.

HERA

(*On phone.*) Hello?

> *PHILOMENA tries Chief Big Rose's headdress on her own head and goes to the "window" to examine her reflection.*

(*Disbelieving.*) No Premier Bob? (*Pause.*) Brian Mulroney is coming instead?!

> *Hearing this, PHILOMENA whips around to HERA and says, (à la Natalie Wood as Maria in "West Side Story"):*

PHILOMENA

Madre de dios. Please, let it not be true.

> *Blackout.*

Scene Ten: The Espanola Hotel

> *Song: "Lookin' For Love"*
>
> *On "stage" of the bar at the Espanola Hotel. EMILY, LIZ and PUSSY are snapping their fingers to a jazz beat and singing sultrily (à la Peggy Lee in "Fever"). ANNIE and FRITZ sit at a beer table watching them.*

EMILY/LIZ/PUSSY

(*Singing.*) "I'm takin' a stroll,
Through the hot streets of town;
While it's high July,
And the sun's beamin' down;
I'm searchin' for feelin's
That I hope will be fine;
And God only knows
If they'll ever be mine;

I'm lookin' at the people,
I'm lookin' all around me,
God I'm lookin' for love
God I'm lookin' for love
God I'm lookin' for …

Lookin' at the people,
And I'm lookin' for love.

"Well, I'm lookin' for love,
On the streets of this town,
Yes, I'm lookin' for love,
On the streets of this town."

Instrumental break.

FRITZ

(*Speaking.*) See him, Annie? See him sittin' over there?
(*ANNIE nods.*) That's Ernie Fingerstein, President of
Mauve Moccasin Records, the little record label that
come outta nowhere—Hamilton, Ontario!—six number
one hits in the past year alone and you can bet there's ...

ANNIE

Oh, I hope he's planning on offering them piles of
money ...

*In the background, EMILY is exhorting the audience
with a hat-as-collection-plate as, in the background,
LIZ and PUSSY snap their fingers and hiss and
whisper to the rhythm of a drum kit going, "poom,
poom, prrrroom, poom ... " (as in Peggy Lee's
"Fever").*

EMILY

Come on, come on, come on, don't be stingy.

FRITZ

When he comes over to our table, don't say nothing.

ANNIE

What do you mean, don't say nothing?

FRITZ

You heard me.

ANNIE

Fritz, the motorcycles in this magazine start at 20,000
bucks a piece.

FRITZ

You'll screw it up. You don't know how to talk to people, like, important white people, like, you don't … you just don't have the right kind of personality.

Humiliated, ANNIE bursts into tears and zooms across the little "dance floor" area and in what she takes to be the "door" to the "washroom." FRITZ merely shrugs her off.

EMILY

(*To audience.*) Remember, folks, this is a fund-raiser for one fancy chief and one fancy motorcade.

An off-stage cook screams at ANNIE from beyond the "door" she's just entered by accident.

COOK

Out! Out! This no the washroom, this my kitchen! Out!

Even more humiliated, ANNIE comes zooming back out, across the little "dance floor" area, and in another "door."

EMILY/LIZ/PUSSY

(*Singing.*) "Well, night's comin' on,
City lights burnin' bright;
Still I'm walkin' alone,
And I ain't feelin' right;
There's gotta be somethin'
And there's got to be someone;
Who will love me forever,
Like the Earth loves the sun;

I'm lookin' at the people,
I'm lookin' all around me,
God I'm lookin' for love
God I'm lookin' for love
God I'm lookin' for …
Lookin' at the people,
And I'm lookin' for love.

"Well, I'm lookin' for love,
On the streets of this town,
Yes, I'm lookin' for love,

On the streets of this town ... "

*Seductively, they scat, vamp and snake their way off
the "stage" and into the shadows. Fade-out until, in
the darkness, all we hear are their finger snaps and
"hisses" and the drums going "poom, poom, prrroom,
poom; poom, poom, prrroom, poom, etc. ... "*

Scene Eleven A: The Keechigeesik's Bedroom

Song: "The Kitchen Rhythm Band" (as background)

*High above, ROSABELLA walks on with her
moon/heart, "pastes" into the night sky, and then
walks off. Down below, a "bed" appears stage right
where lie HERA and ZACHARY, both looking up at the
ceiling. Zachary's "Kitchen Rhythm Band(-to-be)"
plays faintly in the background.*

ZACHARY

Can't sleep, cupcake? (*Silence.*)

HERA

Today. At the store. Big Joey. Picks up one of my flyers
and he reads it to Batman—Manitowabi—across the
counter: "Save the Community Hall for the Homemakers
of Wasy." "Yeah, right," he says to Batman, "Cut their
boobs off and bury them *under* the Community Hall, is
more like it." (*Enraged.*) What is wrong with that man?
What is wrong with ... with ... men? (*Long silence. Then*):

ZACHARY

Cupcake. What would you think if I were to start ... a
kitchen rhythm band?

HERA

A kitchen rhythm what?

ZACHARY

You see, I'd round up as many men as I could from
around here. I'd give them each two pieces of kitchen
equipment from my bakery—pots and pans, ladles,

rolling pins—to reach ... the woman within. They'd bang them together in a musical sort of rhythm, like in an orchestra. Heck, I'd even write the music myself. And the lyrics to these songs, well ... (*Pause.*)

HERA

(*Amused, charmed.*) Well? What about these lyrics?

> ZACHARY *reaches under his pillow, pulls out a rolling pin and cake pan.*

ZACHARY

Hmmm, let's see now. (*Bangs the utensils rhythmically.*) Picture a roomful of male chauvinists going ... (*Sings.*) "We are the kitchen rhythm band, we express our feelings cuz we're not afraid of them, da, dee-dee-da, dee-dee-da, dee-dee-da ... " (*Speaks.*) Something like that.

HERA

(*Laughing.*) Oh, Zachary Jeremiah Keechigeesik. I love you.

> *The sound of the "Kitchen Rhythm Band" crescendos and fades as* ZACHARY *and* HERA *neck passionately,* ZACHARY's *rolling pin and cake pan still in his hands.*

Scene Eleven B: Big Joey's Bedroom

Song: The "Mad Scene" Aria ("Spargi D'Amaro Pianto") from Gaetano Donizetti's "Lucia Di Lammermoor."

High up in the night sky, ROSABELLA *walks on to "turn" her moon/heart a hotter shade of pink, and then walks off. Down below, a second "bed" appears stage left, from which* PUSSY *sits up in a tangle of satiny sheets, brushing her hair playfully in* BIG JOEY's *face. And again,* BIG JOEY *is naked. The aria from t"Lucia di Lammermoor" plays in the background.*

PUSSY

Esposato? Ha dei bambini? Comme pense della gente?

BIG JOEY

And what's that mean?

PUSSY

Are you married? Do you have children? What do you
think of the people?

BIG JOEY

Luciano will be impressed. Where'd you learn Eye-talian?

PUSSY

The winter Liz dragged me to Europe to catch the great
Sophia Sciccolone in her farewell performance of "Lucia
di Lammermoor" at La Scala opera house in Milano.

BIG JOEY

Milano. You're full of surprises, ain't ya?

*He forces her down on top of him, his lips to hers.
PUSSY has to struggle to remain faithful to her
original mission: spying for CHIEF BIG ROSE.*

PUSSY

(*Coy.*) Joe. I gotta know cuz ... cuz of my bookings with
The LaCreams and ... I wanna be by your side when
Luciano gets here ... so ... Guiseppe, mi amore ... when's
he getting here?

BIG JOEY

Week tomorrow. Friday.

PUSSY

But I won't be here.

BIG JOEY

You won't, huh?

PUSSY

We'll be singing in ... Kalamazoo. Michigan, I mean ...
we'll have the night off but ...

BIG JOEY

I could fly you in for the night. Help me with my Eye-
talian. Impress the hell outta Luciano. (*Kisses her, deeply.*)

79

PUSSY
Mmph, so could you?

BIG JOEY
Mmph, could I what?

PUSSY
Fly me in?

BIG JOEY
Of course, babe. But then you're right back on that tour,
ya hear? Cuz things around here? After Luciano? They
ain't gonna be so pretty.

PUSSY tongue kisses him until his eyes roll back.

Oooh, baby. How's that bambini thing go again?

*The Donizetti aria crescendos. And then fades, to be
replaced by a solo cello playing unaccompanied Bach.
And a huge, fat snore.*

Scene Eleven C: The St. Pierre's Bedroom

Song: unaccompanied Bach (on cello).

*In the night sky, ROSABELLA, with ROSETTA by her
side this time, walks on. Together, she and ROSETTA
snap a frill of white around her moon/heart, making
it look like a valentine, then walk off. Down below, a
third "bed" appears stage centre. By the "bed," a
cheap, plastic statue of the Virgin Mary begins to
glow. Crossing herself, VERONIQUE ST. PIERRE is just
rising from kneeling at the statue and putting her
rosary away. She goes to the "bed" and throws the
blanket off to one side, revealing a snoring PIERRE ST.
PIERRE. Both wear long white night shifts and little
white elf caps.*

VERONIQUE
Awus! (*Tries to push him over.*) Sna-ma-bah!

PIERRE

(*Talking in his sleep.*) Creature Nataways! Gimme that gasoline!

VERONIQUE

Get on your side of the bed, you big monkey!

PIERRE

Hup! What're you doing with that lighter gimme that lighter!

> *VERONIQUE bangs PIERRE on the forehead with a fist.*

(*Sitting up, wailing.*) Fire! They're setting my wife on fire! They're burning my wife to an ugly crispy pitch black cinder! (*Sobs.*)

VERONIQUE

Wake up!

PIERRE

(*Awakes gasping.*) Oh, shit la marde, shit la marde! You're alive! You're not dead! Oh, boo-hoo-hoo, boo-hoo-hoo.

VERONIQUE

(*Cooing.*) It's alright, it's alright. It was just a dream. Ohhh, my poor, poor little bag, I'm not on fire at all, there, there.

> *She feels something funny trailing out the front of his night shirt which, as she pulls at it in alarm, gets longer.*

PIERRE

J ... J ... J ... J ... Jealousy Y. Come Again was playing her cello on our front lawn while M ... M ... M ... M ... Munchoos X. Come Again and B ... B ... B ... B ... Big Joey were lounging on lawn chairs, sipping champagne, smoking cigars and playing poker, betting on how high the flames from your corpse were gonna fly, oh, boo-hoo-hoo, boo-hoo-hoo.

> *Turning on a "lamp," VERONIQUE drags a mass of (audio-cassette) tape out of the front of PIERRE's night shirt.*

VERONIQUE

Mary mother of Jesus, what on Earth is this inside your nightshirt?

PIERRE

It's a tape.

VERONIQUE

(*Thrilled.*) *Thee* tape?

PIERRE

No. It's "She Was a Doll" by the LaCreams.

VERONIQUE

(*Furious.*) I told you to get the tape Creature Nataways made of Chief Big Rose promising me a stove, a heart and a place in her motorcade if I got you to vote against Big Joey's casino, not this …

From sheer terror of his wife, PIERRE begins to sob again.

PIERRE

So I got the wrong tape, boo-hoo-hoo, boo-hoo-hoo …

A gunshot resounds outside the window.

VERONIQUE

Mary mother of Jesus, we're being shot at!

PIERRE

Tell 'em we give up! Tell 'em we give up!

VERONIQUE

(*Livid.*) Oh no, we're not.

Diving under the pillow, she resurfaces with a gun and a huge meat cleaver. Outside, footsteps approach. She gives the cleaver to PIERRE and positions herself to shoot while PIERRE sits bolt upright, cleaver at the ready. A dead skunk flies in through a "window" and lands on his knees. They scream. Silence. During which men can be heard outside, laughing and running off. Then VERONIQUE sees the tag tied around the animal's neck.

PIERRE

(*Terrified.*) What's it say?

VERONIQUE

(*Reading tag.*) "Your vote or your wife's a dead skunk."
(*Pause. They look wide-eyed at each other.*) That's it. No
wooden Indian chief, no new stove, no new heart, no
place in the motorcade. If I am going to die, I am going
to die in my own bed like a good Catholic and so, Pierre
St. Pierre, are you.

PIERRE

B ... b ... b ... b ... b ... but what about my job at the new
casino?

VERONIQUE

Simply put, Pierre St. Pierre, you will not vote.

*They look at each other—which one of them will win
in the end?*

Scene Twelve: Gospel Road

Song: Philomena's "Dance of Attack"

*A warm June night, the ROSABELLA moon a soft pink
haze. PHILOMENA MOOSETAIL is walking down
"Gospel Road," carrying the nearly finished pink
Indian chief headdress and her bag of sewing
materials. She hums softly, happily to herself.*

*A MAN wearing a long dark coat appears a distance
behind, following her, PHILOMENA unaware at first.
Gradually, however, his footsteps begin affecting her.
She looks over her shoulder, walks a little faster, a
frenetic, syncopated drumming bleeding in, growing
in intensity as the scene progresses. A SECOND MAN
(CREATURE NATAWAYS) in a dark coat approaches
from her right. She changes direction and walks even
faster. When a THIRD MAN appears on her left, she
changes direction again, almost running now, and
starts talking quietly, nervously, to herself.*

PHILOMENA

Pelajia Rosella Patchnose otherwise known as Chief Big Rose, Emily Dictionary, Liz Jones, Pussy Commanda, where are you when I need you? Why are you following me like this? What have I done to you? Nothing. I've done nothing to you, go away. All I'm doing is minding my own business, all I'm doing is walking home to work on this Indian chief headdress in the luxury of my gorgeous new bathtub after a long hard day helping my sister get the headdresses and bustles ready for her big motor-*cad* for when she receives George Bush who's coming to Wasy in a mere three months in Brian Mulroney's place who's coming in *Premiere* Bob's place because George Bush who's no relation to Nanabush thank god he didn't marry Nana Mouskouri ... (*FOURTH MAN appears.*) ... but anyway George Bush is now coming to meet with my sister to sign over the province of Ontario to the Indians don't ask me why half the time I can't understand what my sister is discussing on the phone with all these big wigs phone phone phone oh I wish I had a phone right now all I know is that it has something to do with the Free Trade Agreement whereby Brian Mulroney might as well have signed the province of Ontario over to George Bush and the Americans, my sister says, which of course is why my sister got mad at Brian Mulroney and cancelled his trip to Wasy ... (*FIFTH MAN appears.*) ... and now wants to see Nanabush I mean George Bush himself might as well get it straight from the horse's mouth, she says, get away get away I know I know I'm going to change direction right here and I'm going to trick them and if I go through Lapatak St. Pierre's old corn field like this I can get to my sister's new hilarium ...

The men appear above, PHILOMENA now surrounded. All five begin closing in on her with exaggerated dance-like movements.

... where I can rest and laugh this whole thing off as a dream, a nightmare a nightmare ooooh get me to that hilarium that hilarium that hilarium I wanna laugh don't wanna cry ... (*Starts to cry.*) ... Help me help me help me help me help meeeeeeeeee!!!!!

The men close in. PHILOMENA shrieks a blood-curdling scream. The "Dance of Attack" begins. One man strips PHILOMENA of her fun fur jacket. A second kicks the sewing paraphernalia out of her hand. The third fights with her over the headdress, finally taking it. CREATURE rips her blouse open, exposing her bra. Her hands fly up to cover herself. Lights change: silhouette of five men beating PHILOMENA with sticks, stones and fists, kicking her as one destroys the headdress completely.

Blackout.

Scene Thirteen: The Study of the Come Again Mansion

Song: unaccompanied Bach (on cello, i.e. recording)

In the study, VERONIQUE stands gazing up at the face of the WOODEN INDIAN CHIEF while, right behind her, PIERRE stands staring at the two pythons inside the "terrarium." A "cello" leans against a chair close by.

VERONIQUE

I know I swore to keep my nose out of this stinking stew of a mess not two days ago ... (*PIERRE pokes her back.*) ... but when Satan himself comes striding onto this reserve, almost killing poor, sensitive Philomena Moosetail ... (*PIERRE pokes her back again.*) ... how can I stand aside and let his actions reign supreme ... (*Another poke.*) ... will you please stop digging into my back?

PIERRE

(*Whispers.*) The tape.

VERONIQUE

(*Turning, thrilled.*) The tape?!

PIERRE

Yes. The one where Chief Big Rose promised you a stove in exchange for my vote against the casino, that's it, I'm sure that's it.

VERONIQUE zooms over to the terrarium and peers inside.

VERONIQUE

Mary Mother of Jesus, it's surrounded by python. (*Horrified silence, then:*) I lift you up, you reach in to get ... (*Gulps back her terror.*) ... the tape.

PIERRE

Uh-uh. *I* lift, *you* reach.

Wide-eyed with horror, they look at each other. Fade-out.

Scene Fourteen: Big Joey's Bedroom

Fade-in on Big Joey's bedroom which, effectively, is now PUSSY's. LIZ is taping a tiny recording device under PUSSY's arm, there to be covered by PUSSY's LaCream's gown.

LIZ

You know it hurts me to even think of your talking to ... well, you know ... (*PUSSY starts speaking in defence but LIZ motions her silent.*) ... I know there's not a thing I can do about your seeing him but ... this time, it's ... dangerous, babe, like life and death. I just wanna make sure you know something: that I love you. I've always ... and ... I'll always be around ... if ... you fall ...

PUSSY now ready for the evening, LIZ kisses her.

Scene Fifteen: Big Joey's Basement and a "Back Road" in Wasy

Song: Luciano's "Tarantella"

At Big Joey's Juke Joint. Sitting around a poker table smoking cigars are BIG JOEY, MUNCHOOS X. COME AGAIN with an exquisitely-coiffed JEALOUSY Y. COME AGAIN and LUCIANO BOCCIA. Beside LUCIANO sits his BODYGUARD, a devastatingly pretty young blond man who has the lean hard look of a killer and, it is subtly obvious, is LUCIANO's lover. CREATURE stands guarding the door. He and BIG JOEY are positioned so that every time BIG JOEY addresses LUCIANO, he can see CREATURE's face hovering directly over and behind LUCIANO's head.

Cross fade to PIERRE and VERONIQUE emerging from the "bushes," the lights of the Come Again mansion aglow in the distance behind them. Carrying the very heavy WOODEN INDIAN CHIEF they've just stolen from the mansion, they shuffle across, far upstage, from right to left.

At the Juke Joint, the men at the table now drink red wine and smoke cigars as a Sicilian tarantella plays in the background. CREATURE watches BIG JOEY's every move, in utter adoration, even mouthing the Italian words after him.

BIG JOEY
(*To LUCIANO.*) Esposato?

Huge pregnant pause. LUCIANO throws a look at his boyfriend who, at this point, is leaning on the arm of LUCIANO's chair, virtually draped over LUCIANO's shoulder.

LUCIANO
Ahem. No. I no married.

BIG JOEY
Ha dei bambini?

*Another uncomfortable pause where LUCIANO's
BODYGUARD shifts in his seat and clears his throat.*

LUCIANO

No. No bambini. Per favore, please. No more questions.

*MUNCHOOS throws BIG JOEY a quick nasty look as
LUCIANO languidly drains his glass. BIG JOEY and
MUNCHOOS then watch LUCIANO's every move as
subtly as they can, though still looking like starving
animals, so badly do they want his money. Finished
drinking, LUCIANO puts his glass down, BIG JOEY
signals CREATURE to get him to refill the glass but
LUCIANO's BODYGUARD beats CREATURE to it. Another
silence during which PUSSY comes elegantly down the
"stairs," nodding to JEALOUSY as she does.*

MUNCHOOS

Signor Boccia, you mentioned, at our last meeting, in
Toronto, that certain conditions had to be met to make
you agreeable to the ... agreement.

LUCIANO

Three conditions.

BIG JOEY

One: the account ...

MUNCHOOS

In Toronto. Is open. The manager ... Roberto
Bombolini? Most willing, to co-operate.

LUCIANO

Bobby Bombolini is eccelente bank manager. And
condition number two, the vote?

*It becomes apparent that the competition between BIG
JOEY and MUNCHOOS for LUCIANO's favour is just
barely under control.*

MUNCHOOS

Monday. Three days from today.

BIG JOEY

Signor St. Pierre's vote? It's in the bag. You have my
word.

LUCIANO

Yes, I am sure the council, it vote for new casino hall, make many people happy.

At this point, the music swells and LUCIANO drifts off into a Sicilian reverie of cigar smoke and red wine. All watch him in silence, breathlessly awaiting his next utterance.

Hand in hand, PIERRE, the WOODEN INDIAN and VERONIQUE dance a tarantella merrily across the downstage area, right in front of the Luciano scene from stage right, the WOODEN INDIAN having the time of its life. At one point, VERONIQUE whips "the tape" (the one they just stole) out of her shoulder-strap purse and, in sheer jubilation, dances with it high in the air. Like Dorothy and her companions in The Wizard of Oz, *the trio dances merrily off stage left.*

Back at Big Joey's, LUCIANO comes out of his reverie.

LUCIANO

And condition number three?

LUCIANO goes off into another reverie. Off-stage, we hear PIERRE and VERONIQUE drop the WOODEN INDIAN, PIERRE screaming in pain, VERONIQUE shushing him. All of which serves to bring the men at Big Joey's back to reality.

MUNCHOOS

I wouldn't worry about it if I were you because ...

BIG JOEY

I have made sure them women know to whom that hall belongs. As for Chief Big Rose ...

MUNCHOOS

I have acquired the means whereby the Chief can be ...

LUCIANO

(*Expectant.*) Can be? ...

MUNCHOOS

Terminated. (*Pause.*) Her ... position.

MUNCHOOS gives a dark look straight into BIG JOEY's eyes. Directly over LUCIANO's head, BIG JOEY looks CREATURE dead in the eye and, as if depending on CREATURE to pull him through for his next statement, says nervously:

BIG JOEY

Signor Boccia. In the end, if Vice-Chief Come Again fails … to reclaim his old job … as Chief, I will terminate the life of said woman. You have my word.

CREATURE nods subtly at BIG JOEY.

PUSSY

Which woman?

BIG JOEY

(*Scowling at her.*) Pelajia Rosella Patchnose. Chief Big Rose. (*Silence.*)

PUSSY

Why? Why would it be necessary to kill Chief Big Rose?

BIG JOEY

(*Exploding.*) Shut the fuck up!

LUCIANO looks up at PUSSY, surprised to hear her speak, amazed that women may actually have brains after all. Taking his blessed time, he talks down to her, as if to a child.

LUCIANO

Because, my sleepy beauty, in my culture, that is the way we are doing … our business, how do you say, incognito, like … spies.

LUCIANO pins PUSSY with the stare of an alligator, making her blood freeze. A knock at the door.

BIG JOEY

(*To MUNCHOOS, low.*) Are we finished here?

LUCIANO nods to MUNCHOOS, he to BIG JOEY, BIG JOEY to CREATURE, who opens the "door" revealing ZACHARY standing there in a baker's hat and frilly pink apron, rolling pin in hand.

ZACHARY

Excuse me, gentlemen but ... I put out a notice some days ago about getting a bunch of guys together for Zachary Jeremiah Keechigeeik's Kitchen Rhythm Band. Now my first class started an hour ago and only three guys showed up but I feel very strongly that you, Big Joey, are in dire need of instruction when it comes to this matter of "misogyny," as they call it. (*Addresses LUCIANO directly.*) But while I'm here, I might as well invite all you guys to join the very first Kitchen Rhythm Band ever to hit the dirt roads of Wasy, what do you say?

Blackout.

Scene Sixteen: The Community Hall

In the darkness, the sound of motorcycles is audible, women's voices shouting to each other above their roar. Then the headlights of these motorcycles glow, as visible through a "window," dancing like fireflies. Lights up on the Community Hall. Both arms in casts, PHILOMENA sits alone, surrounded by the two chief headdresses (pink for her sister, black-and-white for the "dignity-to-appear"), and several partially-completed pow wow dancing bustles. Suddenly, the door flies open and the WOODEN INDIAN CHIEF falls in. PIERRE and VERONIQUE stand at the threshold, panting.

PHILOMENA

Madre de dios, I've been waiting so long for that wooden Indian's head I was beginning to think I might have to have Chief Big Rose's head removed from her shoulders and bronzed.

VERONIQUE

As if I could get another woman on this reserve to help me carry it here. All I've had is Pierre St. Pierre who has a bad back and me with my weak heart ...

PHILOMENA

(*Barks.*) Stand it up. (*The ST. PIERRES jump to it.*) Put the pink one on its head.

> *PIERRE jumps to it—i.e. putting the pink headdress on the WOODEN INDIAN's head—most clumsily, for, distracted by the roar outside, VERONIQUE has zoomed to the "window."*

VERONIQUE

(*Looking out, contemptuous.*) Imagine, Hera Keechigeesik and all those shameless women out there straddling those killer machines ...

> *PIERRE, meanwhile, is mangling the pink headdress.*

PHILOMENA

(*Distressed.*) You're destroying my sister's headdress!

> *VERONIQUE rushes up, shoves PIERRE away, and starts adjusting the headdress on the WOODEN INDIAN's head.*

VERONIQUE

Thank god you have no arms, Philomena Moosetail, so those two viperesses from California can't seduce you into the woman's motorcycle gang they have planned for this reserve, Mary mother of Jesus but at least I have that tape safe and sound right here inside my purse.

> *CHIEF BIG ROSE enters, puffed up with pride.*

CHIEF BIG ROSE

Girls? Here's the new plan.

PHILOMENA

(*In exasperation.*) Not another one!

CHIEF BIG ROSE

Yes, another one. First, I've cancelled George Bush.

PHILOMENA

(*Distraught.*) The headdress.

CHIEF BIG ROSE

Yes, the black-and-white headdress will have to be altered
yet again. Why? I simply took it upon myself to invite
someone more mighty, someone more substantial, more …

PHILOMENA

Who? So I can at least get started.

CHIEF BIG ROSE

Queen Elizabeth!

VERONIQUE

(*Disbelieving.*) No!

CHIEF BIG ROSE

And she promptly agreed. So. I want two hundred of
them dancing bustles lining the main street of
Wasaychigan Hill, Emily and I have agreed that a
motorcade of one hundred motorcycles should do, for I
too shall be riding a motorcycle and, in fact, every
woman on this reserve will be riding one, right up to the
Royal Yacht *Britannia*, whereupon her Majesty and I shall
take the royal quill in hand and sign the treaty giving
Canada back to the Indians, ho-ho!

PIERRE

Holy shit la marde!

*EMILY, LIZ, PUSSY, ANNIE and GAZELLE enter, all
wearing black leather jackets.*

CHIEF BIG ROSE

A-ha! My spies! My motorcade!

*PUSSY takes a Sony walkman from inside her jacket
and pushes the start button. BIG JOEY's taped voice
comes on.*

BIG JOEY

(*On tape.*) Signor Boccia. In the end, if Vice-Chief Come
Again fails … to reclaim his old job … as Chief, I will
terminate the life of said woman. You have my word.

PUSSY

(*On tape.*) Which woman?

BIG JOEY

(*On tape.*) Pelajia Rosella Patchnose. Chief Big Rose.
(*Silence.*)

> *PUSSY clicks the machine off. Silence. All look at*
> *CHIEF BIG ROSE—what will she say? Finally, she*
> *clears her throat.*

CHIEF BIG ROSE

You know, I've lived on this reserve my whole life,
watched generations grow from acorns to oaks, watched
children laugh, men cry, women work, people just plain
refusing to throw in the towel. And all this in the face of
textbooks telling us there was no hope, that we were a
dying race? (*Passionate.*) Hogwash! Just plain hogwash! So
bring on them motorcycles and let's give this Queen
Elizabeth a party such as she has never seen in her life
before!

> *Silence. Followed by a rustle of excitement.*

LIZ

Well then, guess we better get singing so's we can buy
them bikes for one mean motorcade, huh?

GAZELLE

And while we're on tour, Chiefie dear, you got not a
worry cuz motorcade-captain Hera Keechigeesik out
there will be by your side every step of the way. (*Looking*
out the window as the bikes "outside" rev up once more.) Ever
seen a woman ride a Harley like that?

> *Fuse sizzling, a grenade flies in the "window,"*
> *landing right in VERONIQUE's purse. She goes berserk,*
> *everyone screaming. Popping out a "wall," ROSETTA*
> *marches over to VERONIQUE, takes the purse from her*
> *lap, marches across the room, plunks it into PIERRE's*
> *hands and walks back out. All in the room are*
> *mystified. With a shriek, PIERRE jumps and runs out*
> *with the purse. Almost fainting, VERONIQUE crosses*
> *herself.*

CHIEF BIG ROSE

(*Livid, underbreath.*) Oh, they ain't seen nothing yet.

Outside, there is an explosion. Blackout.

Scene Seventeen: The Study of the Come Again Mansion

*In the study, MUNCHOOS X. and JEALOUSY Y. stand
before the terrarium. The atmosphere is poison.*

MUNCHOOS
Where is that tape?

JEALOUSY
(*Quavering.*) I told you, it was right there, between
Marilyn and Arthur.

MUNCHOOS
I see. So one of them swallowed it, is what you're saying.

JEALOUSY
(*Wailing.*) But they wouldn't. They're too well-trained,
they're ...

*MUNCHOOS slaps JEALOUSY hard across the face.
JEALOUSY staggers backwards, knocking her cello over.
MUNCHOOS storms out the room.*

Scene Eighteen A: The Stage of a Bar in Timmins

Song: "Lookin' for Love"

*Wearing funky black ensembles with splashes of
leather, the LaCreams (EMILY, LIZ, PUSSY) sing on
stage. They're working the road, hard. Still, they are
visible and audible, only in a kind of "half-reality,"
as if they were spirits, ghosts, floating through the
land.*

EMILY/LIZ/PUSSY
(*Singing.*) "I'm takin' a stroll,
Through the hot streets of town,
Well, it's high July, etc. ... "

*The "stroll-like" snapping of their fingers (à la Peggy
Lee's "Fever") and their voices (sometimes just
scatting the song) weave their way in and out of the
scenes Eighteen A and B that alternately follow.*

Scene Eighteen B: The Band Council Chambers

Song: "Lookin' for Love"

*At the Band Council Chambers, BIG JOEY and CHIEF
BIG ROSE stand behind podiums at extreme ends of the
stage. The rest address them from the "floor" (i.e. the
audience).*

BIG JOEY

(*To assembly.*) We intend to proceed with this casino *and*
the sale of tax-free cigarettes and gasoline as of Friday,
July 3, 1992. The Minister of Justice cites the Indian Act
as stating: games of amusement may include break-open
ticket games, such as Nevada tickets, and bingo on Indian
territory. But scaling up to casinos interferes with the
province's ability to ensure a level playing field. My
answer? This is Indian land and we, as Native people, can
do with it as we see fit.

ZACHARY

Honourable Chief, I do not disagree with what Mr.
McLeod is saying ...

MUNCHOOS

Mr. Keechigeesik, please wait your turn.

ZACHARY

(*Ramming on.*) It's the methods being used to ram this
crap down the throats of those of us who do not stand to
make a profit from it.

BIG JOEY

Gambling profits mean running water, sewers, schools,
hospitals ...

Scene Eighteen A: The Stage of a Bar in North Bay

Song: "Lookin' for Love"

*The LaCreams continue their song. But this time,
ROSABELLA appears high up above them, singing with
them, effectively now a part of their ghostly, spirit-like
act.*

EMILY/LIZ/PUSSY/ROSABELLA
(*Singing.*) "Well, I'm lookin' for love,
On the hot streets of town,
Yes, I'm lookin' for love, etc. ... "

*Their voices and snapping fingers continue, like
whispers, in the background, an ever-present rhythm.*

Scene Eighteen B: The Band Council Chambers

Song: "Lookin' for Love"

ZACHARY
(*To BIG JOEY.*) So long as th-th-th-th-them casino profits
don't go into lining the pockets of certain unscrupulous,
small-time business*men.*

*In the aisles, VERONIQUE appears sneaking after
PIERRE whose face and head is singed (from the
grenade explosion) and encrusted with melted,
tangled audio-cassette tape.*

VERONIQUE
(*Hissing.*) Pierre St. Pierre!

PIERRE
(*Hissing back.*) Shhh! You're spoiling my concentration. I
gotta vote soon.

*Disgusted with him, VERONIQUE growls and stomps
off.*

CHIEF BIG ROSE

I understand, Vice-Come Again, that you have an ... acquaintance ... named ... Luciano.

MUNCHOOS

I have friends in many places, honourable Chief, I am a well-travelled man. Rome, Paris, London, New York ...

CHIEF BIG ROSE

Well, I myself have a man coming from Sicily to discuss this casino with me. Because when it opens—*if* it opens— I am making it clear, to *him*, that we'll not have them Mafionis meddling with us plain ordinary old Indians. And the man who is flying all the way from Palermo ... (*Aside, to audience.*) ... in place of Queen Elizabeth, whom I just cancelled because she made me mad ... (*Back to normal voice.*) ... flying in all the way from Palermo, Sicily to see me? His name, my dear Vice-Chief, is Signor Vito Corleone.

PHILOMENA

(*Distraught.*) The headdress!

Scene Eighteen A: The Stage of a Bar in Niagara Falls

Song: "Lookin' for Love"

The LaCreams and ROSABELLA *continue their song.*

EMILY/LIZ/PUSSY/ROSABELLA

(*Singing.*) "Well, night's comin' on,
City lights burnin' bright,
Still I'm walkin' alone, etc. ... "

Their voices and snapping fingers continue, like whispers, in the background, an ever-present, underpinning rhythm.

Scene Eighteen B: The Band Council Chambers

Song: "Lookin' for Love"

BIG JOEY

The moment has arrived, honourable Chief, where we
shall let the Council listen to a tape wherein you speak to
a certain Signora St. Pierre of a stove, a heart, a place of
favour in a certain motorcade. Vice-Chief Come Again?

> *CHIEF BIG ROSE blanches. Fortunately for her,*
> *MUNCHOOS frantically signals BIG JOEY that he*
> *doesn't have the tape, whereupon BIG JOEY's face goes*
> *red.*

Well then. On to my next point. I guess. What's all this ...
this fuss about the women losing their Community Hall?
We're only using it for four months, max, by which time a
brand new building will be up—(*Pointedly, at PIERRE.*)
Want a job? (*Back to audience.*)—and *then* the girls will
have their hall back.

HERA

(*Bitter.*) We are *not. You* are going to turn it into a
permanent bingo hall. (*Murmurs of outrage.*)

CHIEF BIG ROSE

My people! (*Murmurs continue.*) My people! (*Murmurs*
continue. She bangs her hammer on the podium.) Will you
please listen to me? (*Murmurs stop.*) Well now, if the vote
should go for this casino, then certain people will get
very, very rich. But what we all stand to lose is our sense
of community, our culture, our soul as a people. That
said, I offer one last morsel of advice before I go and
place my X on the ballot: owning 3 yachts, 7 swimming
pools, 12 BMW's, 832 shirts, 2,179 pairs of shoes, none of
these things ever made Howard Hughes, Christina
Onassis, *or* Elvis Presley happy. Thank you.

> *Blackout.*

Scene Eighteen A: The Stage of a Bar in Windsor

Song: "Lookin' for Love"

The girls bloom forward with the coda of their song. This time, however, ROSABELLA is right there on the stage with them, the other LaCreams singing backup to her lead.

EMILY/LIZ/PUSSY/ROSABELLA
(*Singing.*) "Well, I'm lookin' for love,
On the streets of this town,
Yes, I'm lookin' for love,
On the streets of this town, etc ...

They scat, hiss, snap and conga-line/vamp their way right up to the "voting booth" in the Band Council Chambers. With an elbow each, they lean seductively on the "voting booth" to watch as ... Freeze. Silence.

Scene Eighteen B: The Band Council Chambers

Pin spot on the singed and tape-encrusted PIERRE ST. PIERRE, stepping up to the "voting booth," taking pencil in hand, and aiming. (For him, of course, the LaCreams are invisible; they do not exist.)

PIERRE
(*To audience.*) I don't care what they say in the history books about Pierre St. Pierre, I'm voting and there ain't one single goddamn thing you or anyone who looks like you can do about it. Bleah! (*Votes.*)

Blackout.

Scene Nineteen: The Community Hall

Song: "Movin' Out, Movin' In"

A reggae rhythm starts. At the Community Hall, ZACHARY stands conducting, with a rolling pin-as-baton, a pathetically small group of men who are banging pots and pans, cheese graters and whisks, butcher knifes and cleavers, etc., to the rhythm of the beat, i.e. Zachary's Kitchen Rhythm Band is in rehearsal. ZACHARY himself wears a white chef's hat and frilly pink apron, as do the men in the "band:" PIERRE ST. PIERRE, FRITZ THE KATZ, one other. The "music" stops.

ZACHARY

Lordy, lordy, lordy, that was most excellent to the ears, most, most excellent. Now as you know, Pierre St. Pierre, the women are getting ready for the motorcade that's gonna escort Chief Big Rose to meet Pope John Paul Two when he arrives here in Wasy to sign all of *North America* back to the Indians. Chief Big Rose, of course, was negotiating for South America as well, seeing as this is the year 1992 , but the Catholic foothold in those parts was just too strong so all we're getting is North America, lordy, lordy, lordy. Anyways, when it came to that part of the negotiations where the Holy Father asked if our folks could greet him in traditional Indian costume, the women decided to get the motorcade all decked out in black leather, with fringes of course, for the classical Cree-Ojibway effect. All this by way of explaining that the reason for these benefit concerts in Espanola, Sagamok and Whitefish Lake is so's we can buy all that black leather. So, if you don't mind me asking, Pierre St. Pierre, but can you please play that cheese grater with a bit more oomph?

PIERRE nods humbly, the reggae rhythm resumes, ZACHARY resumes conducting with his rolling pin, and the men start "playing." All this as ...

Around them, the women (VERONIQUE, HERA,
PHILOMENA, GAZELLE, ANNIE, EMILY, LIZ, PUSSY)
enter and start moving the two Indian chief
headdresses and the several pow wow dancing bustles
out of the hall and off-stage in one long conga-line.
As they go, they sing a lamenting "vocalise" over the
men's voices, their dance-like movements gradually
beginning to make them, with their giant splashes of
multi-coloured feathers (on the headdresses and
bustles), resemble Las Vegas chorus girls.

WOMEN
    (*Singing.*) "Oh, oh-oh-oh; oh, oh-oh-oh, etc. ... "

ZACHARY'S MEN
    (*Singing.*) "When I was a little boy here in the
Wasaychigan,
Oh my dear Wasaychigan, the penny, nickel, dime and
dollar
Factor wasn't centre of the universal order of our
Lives, at least the way that I recall them olden days to be
One, then the people actually talked to one another and
they
Visited and they chatted and just generally got along
which I
Think is what the mighty Gitche Manitou intended for
the
People of this beautiful Manitoulin Island for;
One, and you prayed that you and your little children
might have
Chances for a life with minimal pain and minimal hate
and all those
Irritating troublesome degenerate enthusiasm-
Killing consequences, three, four,
Now you can't even live nachur-
Lee, which is sad, which is kinda kinda sad, cuz
This casino's gonna bring about a lotta heartache not the
Least of which is crime and people trusting one another
not.

One, better get the kitchen rhythm section and the
Magic hammer so, three, four, we can
All, two, three, four,
Cool off, two, three, four;
Cuz we're moving' out, we're movin' out, we're moving'
out and we're
Gonna live and love a little less from now
On, two, oh-oh-oh
No, two, three, four."

> *At this point, BIG JOEY and his men (MUNCHOOS,
> CREATURE, LUCIANO'S BODYGUARD, etc.) begin filing
> in carrying "blackjack tables," "slot machines," and
> a roulette wheel, singing in mockery at ZACHARY's
> MEN. And at the WOMEN, who continue their lament
> in even greater earnest. PIERRE, in great shame,
> sneaks over to their side and joins them in their
> singing.*

BIG JOEY'S MEN
> (*Singing.*) "When I was a little boy here in the
> Wasaychigan,
> Oh my dear Wasaychigan, the penny, nickel, dime and
> dollar
> Factor was a piddly little matter that the folks could only
> Dream of as additions to their sad, pathetic little lives
> One, then the people were so poor that such basics as a
> Television, automobile, washing machine, Fridgidaire and
> All these necessary facets were unreachable and of course
> Don't even mention winter holidays in Mexico;
> One, picture me in a fancy great big boat, a
> Cruiser, gliding over glassy lake the summer wind in my
> Hair, semi-naked women, blondes, brunettes and
> redheads
> Draped around my shoulders, three, four;
> Now you can see it all nachur-
> Lee, which is cool, which is kinda kinda cool cuz we
> Beat the daylights outta these the bitches of the world,
> casino
> Here we come we're gonna be rich gonna be the mighty
> ones.

One, blackjack tables, slot machines and wheel of fortune
Roll 'em all in, so, three, four, we can
All, two, three, four,
Cool off, two, three, four,
Cuz we're movin' in, we're movin' in, we're movin' in
and we're
Gonna have a really good time, three, from now
On, two, oh-oh-oh
Yeah, two, three, four."

> *The scene balloons out and then fades, until all the*
> *bustles are gone and the Community Hall is now a*
> *casino, the "roulette wheel" ending up at centre-stage.*
> *The singing voices gradually fading into the distance*
> *outside, the room is now empty of people. Only PIERRE*
> *remains, standing in front of the "roulette wheel"*
> *looking at it with awe. VERONIQUE enters, pokes him*
> *in the back and they hoist up the WOODEN INDIAN*
> *CHIEF and carry it off. Fade-out.*

Scene Twenty: The Community Hall

Song: "Luciano's Tarantella"

At the new Casino/Community Hall, the room sits
empty of people. A tarantella plays in the background.

CREATURE
(*Off-stage.*) Ho-leee! They're lining up straight from here
right up to the outskirts of Manitowaning, look at them
car lights, ho-leee!

> *The front "doors" open and LUCIANO enters with his*
> *BODYGUARD, shown in by MUNCHOOS X. BIG JOEY*
> *and CREATURE follow close behind. LUCIANO sweeps*
> *the room with his alligator glare. The men show their*
> *guest to a blackjack table. All are dressed in tuxedoes.*

LUCIANO
Si. It will do for three months, but for three months only.
Now, I give you money to put up new, bigger building

and ... but ... if you don't do, I will have to deal with
Mama Rosa myself, Signor McLeod, hmmm? Then we will
have good business together, hmmm? And then all the
people of this beautiful island, they work for me and ...
well, they have bright, very bright future, no? (*Silence.*)

MUNCHOOS
(*To BIG JOEY.*) Well? Frilly Face?

BIG JOEY
Right.

> *Blackout.*

Scene Twenty-One: The Hilarium

*Song(s): "When Children Sleep," Rosetta's "Hurdy-
Gurdy," "Apache Chants" and "Keespin Kisagee-in"*

*In the hilarium, CHIEF BIG ROSE, PHILOMENA, EMILY
and LIZ stand looking forlornly out the "window" at
the "twinkling lights" of Wasy far below. Behind them
stands the WOODEN INDIAN CHIEF, with HERA,
GAZELLE, VERONIQUE and ANNIE close by. Only half
of ROSABELLA's heart hangs visible in the sky above
the village. Last, an audio-cassette tape sits on the
"stand" where once stood the avocado plant.*

LIZ
Damn! Damn, damn, damn, damn, damn, we coulda
done it. We coulda stopped 'em if only Pierre St. Pierre
hadna been sucked in by that ... pig. And now we're
going on tour tomorrow. Some spies we've been, huh,
Chief? (*Silence.*)

PHILOMENA
The lights of the new casino ... (*Stops, realizes she's touched
a raw nerve, then continues.*) ... look so pretty from your
hilarium, Pelajia.

CHIEF BIG ROSE

Harumph! Well, there's nothing pretty about what's
going on down there right now, I'll tell you that much.
It's no wonder my hilarium hasn't been working lately.
I'm beginning to wonder if it will ever work again.
(*Silence.*)

> *In the background, women begin singing the backup
> vocals to the song, "When Children Sleep" (i.e. the
> "lullaby" part of it) as though it were coming from
> the women of the village down the "hill." Starting
> very faintly, they grow as* LIZ's *speech progresses.*

LIZ

You know, one summer, me and Pussy Commanda, we
rode our bikes to Oklahoma, Anadarko, Oklahoma, south
of Oklahoma City. Indian City, U.S.A., they call it. That's
where she's from, Pussy Commanda. She's Apache, with
some Kiowa and white. They say the Anadarko pow wow
is the biggest in the world.

PHILOMENA

Listen. The women of Wasy are singing their children to
sleep.

> *The women listen for a moment, entranced. Then
> their attention goes respectfully back to* LIZ.

LIZ

Anyway. Dancers from all over North America come there
every August, to dance, from sunrise to sunset. But—and
it's the strangest thing you ever saw—they have this
fairground there, right behind the pow wow grounds.
And as the day wanes, the Elders—all these ancient men
and women, Apache, Commanche, Kiowa, Wichita,
Cheyenne, Cherokee, Yakima, Seneca, you name it—they
bring their lawn chairs and they set them down all
around the edge of that fairground and there they wait
for the sun to set. And the fairground comes to life:
merry-go-rounds, Ferris wheels, the Spider, the Wildcat,
all these rides, their lights come on. And the music from
them ...

Merry-go-round music comes on in the background,
provided by ROSETTA DICTIONARY's hurdy-gurdy as
she "hovers" up above the roulette wheel in the new
casino, ROSABELLA JEAN BAEZ standing lovingly by
her side, the roulette wheel coming alive with
twinkling lights and turning ... effectively the Ferris
wheel LIZ is speaking of.

... from where I stood, I could see these seven ancient
Apache men sitting, drinking, dancing around this one
picnic table between me and the fairground. And these
men, they were playing hand drums and chanting, these
timeless Apache chants ...

The voices of old men chanting a pow wow chant
starts playing in the background, weaving in and
out of the merry-go-round music.

... circus music, circus lights ... and Apache chants
30,000 years old. It was like hearing the Earth singing,
breathing, wheezing out its last gasp, against the fumes of
this ... trivial, meaningless ... light, the slow death of an
entire nation, the slow death of ... the Earth ...

The light on ROSETTA fades out but the sound of her
hurdy-gurdy (i.e. the fairground music) continues,
until it too fades away.

EMILY

I wish they'd shut up. I wish those women out there
would just shut up.

PHILOMENA

No, Emily. All children sleep. Some for the night, some
forever ...

CHIEF BIG ROSE

It doesn't have to be like this, does it? Our children don't
have to die?

In the dimness, a candle flame pops up. Eerily feeling
ROSETTA's presence in the room, EMILY begins to
weep. PHILOMENA puts an arm around her shoulder,
giving EMILY the strength to sing "When Children
Sleep." ROSETTA's presence is indicated, at first, by

this single candle flame which seems to "float"
around the set, as if on its own, until, later on in the
sequence, it becomes evident that the candle is
actually being carried around by ROSETTA herself, as
the "ghost child" walks about, in almost ceremonial
fashion. The lights isolate EMILY and all else—but
EMILY and ROSETTA-in-candle-flame, that is—seems
to fade into mere shadows.

EMILY
 (*Reciting, over women humming their lullaby.*)
 "When children sleep, their bodies lie at rest,
 But they are not at rest, they travel,
 They travel the length and the width of rooms, the
 children,
 They travel the length and the width of houses, the
 children,
 The length and the width of the Earth and more;
 And on these travels, who knows what they see, the
 children;
 Do they see the stuff of which the walls of houses are
 made?
 Do they see the substance of the moon, the way this
 Earth is made of soil and rock and magic molecules,
 The way the human soul is made of spider's webs and
 veins and blood that glistens in the sun?
 They see all this, I do believe, and more,
 When children sleep."

  For the chorus, the women join EMILY in multi-part
  harmony.

EMILY AND WOMEN
 (*Singing.*) "When children sleep,
 They fly by the moon as they leap
 In the night;
 Away to the end of the eternal light,
 Away … "

  For the second verse, the women go back to their
  humming of the lullaby under EMILY.

EMILY

"When my baby sleeps, oh the night away, oh the night
away, oh-oh,
She begins to glow, like the candle flame, like the candle
flame, oh-oh;
In the dark of life, such a darkness there, oh the darkness
there, oh-oh;
I reach out and touch, but my baby's gone, oh my baby's
gone, oh-oh;
Please don't leave me here, oh my baby dear, oh my baby
mine, oh-oh;
Feel so all alone, don't know what to do, don't know what
to do, oh-oh;
Sitting in the dark, holding out my hand, holding out my
hand, oh-oh;
Where do children go, when they go to sleep, where do
children go, oh-oh;
Spirit having flown, to the sky above, oh the sky above,
oh-oh;
Flickering its wing, in the air above, oh the air so high,
oh-oh;
Looking at the light, oh the light above, oh the light so
high, oh-oh;
Oh the holy light, oh the light of God, oh the light of
God, oh-oh;
Why can't I go there, with my baby dear, oh my baby
mine, oh-oh;
Please come back to me, oh my baby dear, oh my baby
mine, oh-oh;
But my baby's gone, oh my baby's gone, oh my baby
mine, oh-oh;
And I'm all alone, oh so all alone, oh so all alone ... "

> *ROSETTA comes right up to EMILY. EMILY takes her in
> his arms and hugs her deeply. (And again, the multi-
> part harmony for the chorus resounds).*

EMILY AND WOMEN

(*Singing.*) "When children sleep,
They fly by the moon as they leap
In the night;

Away to the end of the eternal light,
Away …
Away to the end of the eternal light,
Away … "

(*Speaking, lovingly, to ROSETTA.*) Rosetta.

> *EMILY opens her arms and smiles at the child, as if memorizing every detail of her face. All the women exit from the hilarium.*

ROSETTA
(*Singing, quietly, to EMILY.*) "Keespin kisagee-in, seemak kaweecheewin; if you love me, you will come with me … "

EMILY
(*Speaking.*) Not yet, my baby, not yet. Mommy's still got a shit loada work left to do.

> *ROSETTA smiles lovingly once more at her mother. Then EMILY lets her go. Her lit candle still in hand, the little girl "floats" up to the moon where ROSABELLA awaits her. As she approaches, ROSABELLA reaches out for her hand. Puff! ROSETTA's candle flame flickers out. And out of it "pops" a small pink heart, thus giving Wasy two moons now, both shaped like hearts, both pink, one large, one small.*

> *And, last, away down below, under this soft pink moonlight, bombshell GAZELLE, alone, sashays into Chief Big Rose's hilarium. With elegant stealth and, to just a hint of the jazz beat from the song, "Lookin' for Love" (as in, "poom, poom, prrroom, poom"), she takes the audio-cassette tape from the "stand" where it was left by the Chief and sashays out the door.*

GAZELLE
So easy, ah … (*Chuckles throatily and sashays out.*)

> *Fade-out. Except for, away up above, the two pink moon/hearts.*

ACT THREE

Scene Twenty-Two: The Anchor Inn

Song: "Jukebox Lady"

First, ROSETTA's candle flame "hovers" in the air, seemingly all by itself. Then: the bar of the Anchor Inn in Little Current. GAZELLE, BIG JOEY and CREATURE sit at a beer table drinking beer. The music playing on the "jukebox" is "Jukebox Lady" as recorded by the LaCreams (EMILY doing solo, LIZ and PUSSY doing backup).

EMILY/LIZ/PUSSY

(*On jukebox, singing.*) "She is the Jukebox Lady,
She dances through the light,
Of pale, pink-coloured dreams,
Her eyes white flames in the night;
Hey there, Ojibway lady,
Your time's not here it seems;
Those far away tomorrows,
Remain but soft-coloured dreams ... "

As she sings along to the jukebox, GAZELLE, stretching like a cat, provocatively slips the cassette tape she stole from Chief Big Rose's hilarium at the end of Act Two out of her back jeans pocket and wedges it into her cleavage.

111

GAZELLE

(*Singing along.*) " ... Those far away tomorrows,
Remain but soft-coloured dreams."

(*Speaking.*) Oh god, I wanna be a LaCream, I wanna be a
LaCream, please God, let me be a LaCream, I wanna be
famous, I wanna be rich, I wanna shop till I drop ...

CREATURE

Ho-leee, what's that tape doing sticking outta your tit
crack?

GAZELLE

(*Gasps.*) Oh! (*Coy.*) Now that you mention it ... (*Slips tape
out and holds it out to BIG JOEY, seductively.*) ... you know,
we're on our way to Memphis—Tennessee—Fritz and the
girls. And me, their dresser. Friday night, Beale Street,
B.B. King's Emporium. And when we get back, I expect to
land right back in your arms. Again. So while I'm gone,
pooch, have a listen. To this. Guaranteed, you'll love it.

*Blackout. Except for ROSETTA's candle flame, away
up above.*

Scene Twenty-Three: Big Joey's Basement

Song: unaccompanied Bach (cello)

*In Big Joey's basement, PUSSY, MUNCHOOS and an
exquisitely-groomed JEALOUSY Y. COME AGAIN sit
having drinks. JEALOUSY wears one of her pythons
around her shoulders as a tape of her cello-playing
(unaccompanied Bach) plays in the background,
coming from the "cassette deck" above the "bar."*

JEALOUSY

(*To PUSSY.*) ... You see, I've always had this dream where
we could be moving, together, into the 21st century, as a
highly sophisticated race of people. I don't know about
you but I've had quite enough of all this talk about the
plight of the poor Indian and the poverty and the
alcoholism and the despair and the suicide. I think that

112

the problem lies in our trying too hard to hang on to "the old way," a culture where moccasins, dream visions and spiritual experiences were the norm, where women had, if not an upper hand, then certainly, at the very least, an equal hand in the way life was lived. We no longer live in an era of matriarchy, however, those days are past. These days, since the arrival of Columbus five hundred years ago this October, we have been living in a patriarchy, a culture where men rule the roost, where women *must* remember to keep their place, quietly, in the background, in the home, supporting their men as they go about the business of the world. We Indian people now live in a world of technology and high finance, which is why this new casino could do us so much good. Why, we could eventually have our own symphony orchestra, our own ballet company, and do away with those out-dated tom-toms and primitive dances at the pow wow ...

> BIG JOEY enters and stands there waving a cassette tape in the air, looking straight at PUSSY, with rage. He grabs PUSSY roughly by the collar and lifts her off her seat. Struggling, PUSSY tries to peel his hands off her blouse.

PUSSY

Ow! Don't do that! Let go!

> BIG JOEY bangs PUSSY viciously back into her seat and slaps the cassette tape down on the table. MUNCHOOS and JEALOUSY exchange a hurried little look, then begin leaving. In the deafening silence (the Bach tape is going on automatic switch-over), BIG JOEY stares flames into PUSSY's eyes while PUSSY sits paralysed with terror. The sound of Zachary's Kitchen Rhythm Band can be heard briefly in the far distance.

> As BIG JOEY's and PUSSY's scene progresses, MUNCHOOS and JEALOUSY cross the stage arm in arm, the screaming voices of BIG JOEY and PUSSY audible behind them. JEALOUSY having forgotten her tape, her cello-playing resumes.

BIG JOEY

You've been spying on me, haven't you?

PUSSY

What are you talking about?

BIG JOEY

Don't lie to me.

PUSSY

I am not lying.

BIG JOEY

You know what I do to women who lie to me?

> *BIG JOEY pulls back to punch PUSSY's face with*
> *incredible force. Blackout. In the darkness, the punch*
> *sounds like a rock hitting a brick wall. PUSSY wails*
> *out with agony. The punches and the screams fade*
> *into the background as the sound of JEALOUSY's cello-*
> *playing blooms into the foreground, lyrical, heart-*
> *rending. There is no moon in the sky, only ROSETTA's*
> *candle flame, away up above.*

Scene Twenty-Four: Memphis Dressing Room

> *In their dressing room at B.B. King's Emporium in*
> *Memphis, Tennessee, EMILY and LIZ are preparing*
> *feverishly for their appearance on stage. GAZELLE is*
> *helping them with their wigs, gowns (black), opera*
> *gloves, etc. ANNIE clumsily tries to help with make-up,*
> *false eyelashes, etc., but mostly just gets in the way.*
> *And FRITZ is on the telephone frantically arguing*
> *with somebody.*

FRITZ

So where the hell is she?

LIZ

I'm never talking to her again.

EMILY

Bitch.

ANNIE

Right. I wouldn't talk to her even if she was wearing a cat's costume.

EMILY, LIZ and GAZELLE stop in their tracks to look at ANNIE, surprised at her sudden assurance.

FRITZ

(*On telephone, beyond himself with rage.*) She was supposed to be on that 10 o'clock flight from Detroit, last night. I even went ...

All FRITZ has to do is to motion ANNIE to light his cigarette for her to jump to it.

GAZELLE

(*Doing voice warm-up.*) Me-me-me-me-me-me-me-me-me. Moo-moo-moo-moo-moo-moo-moo-moo-moo ...

FRITZ

Well, fuck you then, Mr. Joseph Jeremiah McLeod. (*Bangs phone down.*) Jeeeeeesus fuckin' Joseph Mary Peter John and all them other fuckin' goddamn son-of-a-bitch apostle saints thrown in! (*Grabs PUSSY's black gown and throws it at ANNIE.*) Annie. Throw this on.

ANNIE

(*Horrified.*) You want me to ...

FRITZ

Annie. Don't fuck with me. (*Sings.*) "White boys fall in love ... " (*Speaks.*) Come on. Come on, come on, come on, come on, come on, *come on*!!!

ANNIE

(*On the verge of tears.*) I need to practice it.

FRITZ

(*Livid.*) Get out there and sing you pathetic little jerk!

LIZ

(*Deadly.*) She said no. (*Long, dangerous silence.*)

GAZELLE

(*Dead calm, then seductive as hell.*) I do harmonies. I know the songs. (*Coyly producing a black dress from behind her.*) And wouldn't ya know it but I just happened to squeeze

in a little bit of shoppin' ... (*Cold, to FRITZ.*) ... at our stop
back in Toledo. (*Silence.*)

EMILY

(*Gently.*) Annie. Go on out there and do "The Place
Where I Belong," won't you? We have no choice. We
gotta go on. Gazelle needs time to get dressed and
made-up and ... One song, please?

ANNIE

(*Mortified.*) Emily, I can't. I can't go out there by myself.
I ...

EMILY

(*With immense love.*) You won't be by yourself. By the time
you hit that second chorus, we'll be right there behind
you. You can do it, Annie.

> *Blackout. Except for ROSETTA's candle flame, away
> up above.*

Scene Twenty-Five: On Stage at B.B. King's Emporium

Song: "The Place Where I Belong"

*On stage at B.B. King's Emporium, ANNIE stands
alone in a pool of light, mike in hand, head hanging
down over her chest. When the intro to the song, "The
Place Where I Belong," begins, she slowly brings her
head up. At first, she is terrified but as the song picks
up, gains confidence until, by the end, she is
positively sensational.*

ANNIE

(*Sings, torch-song style.*) "Oh-oh-oh ...
Who the hell did ever say that lovin' and a-livin'
Took a whola lotta catchin' and a-chasin' of the chilly
hearted?
All that a-huggin' and a-kissin' and a-neckin' and a-
cookin' all that,

So they tell me, necessary pain and heartache;
Just ain't necessary I don't have to tie my heart
In chain and rope and all that unnecessary jazz,
Cuz I ain't wastin' no cryin'."

> *FRITZ becomes visible standing (or sitting) in the
> front row of the audience, watching ANNIE with, at
> first, sceptical eyes, then with increasing surprise,
> until by the end, he is blown away completely.*

(*Chorus, fast.*) "Been a long time, since I gone
To the place where I belong;
Oh the place where I belong
Is the place where I'm, oh, all alone."

(*Very fast.*) "Oh-oh-oh well-a my-a itty bitty baby bought a
Ticket to the Manitoba city where he says he's gonna live
forevah,
Will-a my-a lovey dovey honey ever take anothah
Mini little poke at lovin' me and not anothah;
Even if he doesn't ever take another look at me,
Even if he doesn't ever breathe another word at me,
I ain't wastin' no cryin'."

ANNIE/EMILY/LIZ/GAZELLE

> (*The latter three not seen at first.*)
> "Been a long time, since I gone
> To the place where I belong;
> Oh the place where I belong,
> Is the place where I'm, oh, all alone."

> *EMILY, LIZ and GAZELLE become visible only by the
> end of the above chorus.*

ANNIE

> (*This time very fast.*) "Oh-oh-oh,
> Who the hell did ever say that lovin' and a-livin'
> Took a whola lotta catchin' and a-chasin' of the chilly
> hearted?
> All that a-huggin' and a-kissin' and a-neckin' and a-
> cookin' all that,
> So they tell me, necessary pain and heartache;
> Just ain't necessary I don't have to tie my heart

In chain and rope and all that unnecessary jazz,
Cuz I ain't wastin' no cryin'."

ANNIE/EMILY/LIZ/GAZELLE

(*Chorus.*) "Been a long time, since I gone
To the place where I belong;
Oh the place where I belong
Is the place where I'm, oh, all alone."

> *During this last statement of the chorus, we see the*
> *faint glimmer of fourteen pow wow dancing bustles*
> *moving—rustling like magic birds—from the wings*
> *on both sides of the stage and toward centre stage.*
> *And a company of voices faintly singing, as in the*
> *distance, below and with the* ANNIE/EMILY/
> LIZ/GAZELLE *"chorus" as above.*

COMPANY

(*Singing.*) "Jesus is a-comin' home,
To the place where he belongs; (*Shouting.*) Yes, Jesus!
(*Singing.*) Oh, the place where he belongs
Is this place where he'll feel right at home."

> *At B.B. King's Emporium,* ANNIE's *song comes to a*
> *spectacular finish, the applause deafening,* FRITZ
> *clapping and shouting loudest of all, seemingly*
> *unable to stop. Fade-out. During this fade-out, the*
> *"ghost" of Elvis Presley "hovers" in the air above the*
> *girls for one fleeting second, for all intents and*
> *purposes, an optical illusion. In the blackout, the*
> *only thing left visible is* ROSETTA's *candle flame.*

> *The lights flash on and we are back in Wasy. The*
> *entire community bursts onto the stage, bustles in*
> *hand, waving them and singing, full out this time—*
> *in hair-raising, foot-stomping gospel fashion. As they*
> *sing, they come to hang the bustles in two lines on*
> *either side of Wasy's "main road."*

COMPANY

(*Singing.*) "Jesus is a-comin' home,
To the place where he belongs ... (*Shouting.*) Yes, Jesus!
(*Singing.*) Oh, the place where he belongs
Is this place where he'll feel right at home."

*During the instrumental break here (the verse form of
the song), CHIEF BIG ROSE appears at centre-stage,
speaking with the zeal of an evangelical preacher. All
as the women come rolling "motorcycles" on and
proceed to line both sides of Wasy's main road with
them, right under the two lines of pow wow dancing
bustles.*

CHIEF BIG ROSE

(*Speaking.*) Yes, Jesus is a-comin', I know he's a-comin', he
told me so himself! He's a-comin' down from his home
up in the sky right here to Wasaychigan Hill to return the
world to us! (*Aside to the audience.*) I cancelled the Pope,
ha-ha! (*Back to evangelical fervour.*) Yes, Jesus is a'comin'
home to give the world back to the Indians!

COMPANY

(*Singing.*) "Jesus is a-comin' home,
To the place where he belongs ... (*Shouting.*) Yes, Jesus!
(*Singing.*) Oh, the place where he belongs
Is this place where he'll feel right at home."

Blackout.

Scene Twenty-Six: Big Joey's Basement

*The outlines of the ROSABELLA and ROSETTA
moon/hearts glow pink in the night sky above the
twinkling lights of the village of Wasaychigan Hill.*

*In Big Joey's basement, CHIEF BIG ROSE sits with BIG
JOEY on the chaise longue, the only piece of furniture
left in the room other than the coffee table in front of
them on which sits a bottle of wine. On their best
behaviour, they are just toasting each other and,
finished taking their first sip, put their glasses down
on the coffee table.*

CHIEF BIG ROSE

Do you know, Big Joey, I was thinking of cancelling Jesus.

BIG JOEY

(*Certain she's finally "lost it."*) Cancelling Jesus, hmm-humm?

CHIEF BIG ROSE

You see, I was thinking that it might be a bit much to expect ... the world when ... well, I just don't want the Indians to be disappointed, if you know what I mean. Now, the girls, as you know, have been very successful with their singing and all that ... glittery ... whatever. In fact, when they were in Memphis just two weeks ago, their show was attended one night by none other then the great Elvis himself, as you might have read in the *National Enquirer*. So impressed, in fact, was the King of Rock and Roll that he went backstage afterward to offer them the use of his mansion, what is it called again? Raceland? Placeland?

BIG JOEY

Graceland.

CHIEF BIG ROSE

Thank you. Anyway, he let them know that he felt the property rightfully belonged to the Indians, as it rests on ancient Cherokee territory. So I was thinking that, for your big, big, really big casino opening on the first of September is it, now? ... (*BIG JOEY nods.*) ... that I might get the girls to invite him up for your grand opening, as your very special guest. After all, we now have 121 motorcycles and 300 of them pow wow dancing bustles to line the main road of Wasaychigan Hill.

BIG JOEY

Yes, but why are you ...

CHIEF BIG ROSE

Now the girls, as you yourself must know, are ending their current tour at Caesar's Palace in Las Vegas, in fact, their final show there happens to be August 31st, wouldn't you know it, and I'm sure I could talk them into bringing that very same show in for at least one more performance, that is, if you don't have another band already arranged ...

BIG JOEY

As a matter of fact I …

CHIEF BIG ROSE

I'll cancel them. (*Silence. They eye each other balefully.*) That is, if that's agreeable with you.

BIG JOEY

Well, it's not actually that simp …

CHIEF BIG ROSE

I have issued orders—to *my* people, now that your casino is here to stay—to throw their support behind it for we, as a community, must work together for the betterment of all, don't you agree that this is a wise decision on my part?

BIG JOEY

Yes, but I'm still curious as to why the motorcy …

CHIEF BIG ROSE

(*Banging her glass down and rising.*) Very well. Then I shall return post haste, as my son Tom would say, to my office to place the necessary calls.

BIG JOEY

Fine. (*Rises.*)

CHIEF BIG ROSE

(*Extending hand and smiling.*) I look forward to a most robust and enthusiastic collaboration.

> BIG JOEY *looks stunned as she robustly shakes his hand. As she begins to leave,* PUSSY COMMANDA *can just be heard moaning in an adjoining room.*

PUSSY

(*Off-stage, in immense pain.*) Joe?

> CHIEF BIG ROSE *pauses for one split second to register this, shoots* BIG JOEY *a look, and then exits, deep in thought. Fade-out.*

Scene Twenty-Seven: Main Road of Wasy

Song: "White Boys Fall in Love" (intro only)

In the darkness, the bass line of the song, "White Boys Fall in Love," begins, underscoring the next scene. There is a flurry of excitement: voices babbling, etc. When the lights come up, we are on the main road of Wasy, which is still lined with "motorcycles" and pow wow bustles. People begin arriving, formally dressed, on their way to the casino grand opening, among them the ghosts of ROSETTA and ROSABELLA (still in her feathered, showgirl outfit, still looking like a fabulous bird of paradise). At centre-stage, BIG JOEY presents CHIEF BIG ROSE to "dignitaries" as they enter in a kind of "receiving line."

BIG JOEY
Mayor of Espanola.

CHIEF BIG ROSE
Great to see you here, Jack.

BIG JOEY
Mayor of Sudbury.

CHIEF BIG ROSE
Teddy, my boy, how was your holiday?

BIG JOEY
Cardinal of Toronto.

CHIEF BIG ROSE
Aloysius Ambrosic, you old bag. Haven't seen you since you got outta jail.

LUCIANO BOCCIA appears with his BODYGUARD.

BIG JOEY
Luciano Boccia.

CHIEF BIG ROSE
(*Mock quizzical.*) Poochiano Poach what?

PIERRE ST. PIERRE rushes up and practically shoves LUCIANO aside.

PIERRE

About this Manager of Libations business, Big Joey …

BIG JOEY

Not now, Pierre, can't you see I'm busy?

PIERRE

Hup! Don't contribute your elder.

CHIEF BIG ROSE

(*Calling.*) Creature! Creature Nataways! (*To LUCIANO.*)
You'll have to excuse me, Pooch.

> *She makes her way through the crowd. Trying to*
> *avoid PIERRE, BIG JOEY turns to LUCIANO.*

BIG JOEY

Mr. Presley should be arriving any minute now.

PIERRE

(*To BIG JOEY.*) I think it's high falutin' time you and me sat
down and had a little kit kat about that little contrap you
and me signed away back when, which is just a nice way
for me to ask you for some money up front and so, Big
Joey, I hereby takes it upon myself to ask you flat in your
face, no fuss, no mess, boom! Gimme 5,000 dollars.

> *Their conversation fades into the hubbub as that of*
> *CHIEF BIG ROSE and CREATURE NATAWAYS rises to the*
> *foreground.*

CHIEF BIG ROSE

… but she never said nothing to Liz Jones or to Emily
Dictionary and I find that very …

CREATURE

… I tole you once I tole you twice, Chief Big Rose, them
three girls ain't on speakin' terms no more …

CHIEF BIG ROSE

You're sure she went back to California?

CREATURE

Ever nosey, you. Pussy Commanda and Big Joey had one
of them big nasty fights where the toasters was a-flyin'
and the furniture re-arranged …

123

*Their conversation fades into the hubbub as that of
BIG JOEY's and PIERRE's comes back into the
foreground.*

PIERRE

Sold! (*Hugs BIG JOEY madly. BIG JOEY tries to peel him off.*)
Ooooh, wait until my wife hears about this, that new stove
she's been tossin' and churnin' and writhin' and night-
marin' about ... (*Scurries off, calling.*) Hey, little bag! Little
bag! Have you seen my little bag anywhere around ...
(*Disappears into the crowd.*)

LUCIANO

(*To BIG JOEY.*) It look like, perhaps, condition number
three will no longer be necessary, no?

> *MUNCHOOS X. and JEALOUSY Y. COME AGAIN sweep
> imperiously by on their way to the casino "entrance,"
> MUNCHOOS and LUCIANO nodding at each other. BIG
> JOEY cranes his neck to see above the crowd when
> CREATURE NATAWAYS comes running up to him.*

CREATURE

Maybe his plane was late gettin' in, huh, Big Joey? The TV
was sayin' they had all kinds of fog and what not at the
Sudbury airport but chris'sakes, huh, Big Joey, givin'
Graceland back to the Indians? Ho-leee! ...

Scene Twenty-Eight: The New Casino

Song: "White Boys Fall in Love"

*Bang! The lights of the brand new Casino Royale
flash on and we are in: "Las Vegas-on-the-Rez!"*

FRITZ

(*On mike.*) Ladies and gentlemen, all the way from
Caesar's Palace, Las Vegas, Nevada, THE U. S. OF A., the
fabulous, the sensational, the unbelievable ... the
LaCreams!

And from the "stage" of the "casino," the LaCreams
appear, looking like a sensational Indian version of
the Supremes: LIZ JONES, EMILY DICTIONARY and ...
GAZELLE NATAWAYS. The crowd goes wild.

EMILY/LIZ/GAZELLE

(*Singing. Chorus.*) "White boys fall in love,
With such fancy toys,
With money, power and cars,
With girls who say 'come hither boys;'
We've got news for you,
We're no fancy toys;
We're worth way more than your cars,
So no thanks to all of you boys."

LIZ

(*Singing, to MUNCHOOS.*) "I once had a drink with this boy,
Who said he would like me to
Pose in diamonds, fur and perfume,
Things I do not do;
Then he took me for a ride,
In his little red sedan,
To his nest of love on Bloor Street,
Where I said good-night to him."

> *Repeat chorus, EMILY doing lead, LIZ and GAZELLE*
> *doing the "baby, babies" under her.*

EMILY

(*Singing, to LUCIANO.*) "I had dinner once with this boy,
Who had so much gold he glowed;
In the candlelight he kissed me,
I was so unmoved;
Then he blew the candle out,
Moonlight rushed in with a roar;
He asked me to reveal my soul,
So right then I walked out that door."

> *Repeat chorus, EMILY doing lead, LIZ and GAZELLE*
> *harmonies, and anonymous, off-stage men's voices*
> *doing the "baby, babies" under them.*

GAZELLE

(*Singing, to* BIG JOEY.) "I once almost took this ring,
From this boy who wanted me,
For his little wife to be,
Far as I could see;
I held out my hand to take it,
This engagement ring so fine,
Laid my lips upon that diamond,
Then I returned it to him."

Repeat chorus, again with EMILY *on lead,* LIZ *and*
GAZELLE *on harmonies but, this time, it is revealed
that the anonymous men's voices that were doing the
"baby, babies" in the last chorus above are actually
members of Zachary's Kitchen Rhythm Band.
Introduced with a flourish by the ghost of* ROSABELLA,
*five muscular, fair-skinned young men descend from
the rafters on trapezes, dressed in the flimsiest of
bejewelled jock straps and full Las Vegas showgirl
plumage, the colour scheme of which is that of the*
RCMP *uniform. The star attraction in this chorus is*
LUCIANO'*s stunning, hunky blonde boyfriend. A
whole slew of pots, pans, butcher knives, meat cleavers
and other kitchen equipment descends, suspended
above their heads, during the very last statement of
the chorus.*

For this last repeat of the chorus, CHIEF BIG ROSE
*herself is having such a good time that she gets lifted
onto the "stage" from where she starts scatting overtop
all the other voices, looking fabulous in a sequined
gown and waving her famous, silver hammer in the
air.*

Suddenly, a riot breaks out. Led by HERA *and* ANNIE,
*the women, in their evening finery, take their
positions standing on top of "card tables", sitting on
"slot machines," etc. and chasing everyone out the
door. In the foreground,* CHIEF BIG ROSE *walks up to*
LUCIANO, *whips him around and snaps a finger.*

*Photographers, TV cameras and microphones appear
clustered all around them, flash-bulbs exploding.*

CHIEF BIG ROSE
Poochiano Poach Ya? Meet the paparazzi, ha-ha!

*LUCIANO reacts like a vampire to a crucifix. CHIEF
BIG ROSE grabs him by the ear, like a mother with her
little boy, and "drags" him to the "door."*

CHIEF BIG ROSE
I want you and your kind off this reserve and I do not
want you to come back or you will find yourself in very,
very serious trouble, do you hear me? In other words, you
old Sicilian rat, I cancel you.

She "throws" him out. Cross-fade into ...

*During this cross-fade, we hear the sound of
motorcycles revving up and "surrounding" the
casino. And the sound of people rioting.*

Scene Twenty-Nine: The LaCreams' Dressing Room at the Casino

*The LaCreams' dressing room, where the LaCreams
are just rushing in, throwing off their wigs, peeling
off their opera gloves, etc. Excited to near hysteria,
they are practically tripping over each other's words.*

EMILY
She's doing it, she's doing it! Red Lucifer's whiskers, the
old brown bitch is doing it! Blockading the casino.

LIZ
With motorcycles!

GAZELLE
Come on, let's go find our bikes.

LIZ
(*Ripping off her clothes.*) Yeah, yeah, yeah, just gimme time
to get outta this straitjacket.

EMILY

Anyone see Puss out there?

LIZ

(*Cold, still.*) No. (*Silence. They all pause.*)

EMILY

Well, I smell a rat.

> *Behind them, the "door" flies open, and then slams shut. And there stands a terrified JEALOUSY Y. COME AGAIN, her hair and ensemble totally dishevelled— she's just been "trampled" in the riot and this is her only haven.*

Scene Thirty: Outside the Casino

> *The lights of the casino behind them, the sound of motorcycles idling (their headlights visible), CHIEF BIG ROSE and BIG JOEY walk up to each other, as in a duel.*

BIG JOEY

Get these motorcycles outta here.

CHIEF BIG ROSE

This motorcycle blockade, Mr. Joseph Jeremiah McLeod, will remain a motorcycle blockade until such time as,
a) the profits from this casino business do in fact go to education, paved roads, sewers, etc. for this reserve;
b) the criminal element is removed from this casino business and this reserve forever; and,
c) you put a stop to this male violence against women, once and for all. Case closed.

> *Blackout.*

Scene Thirty-One: The LaCreams' Dressing Room at The Casino

In their dressing room, EMILY, LIZ and GAZELLE stand facing a very distraught JEALOUSY Y. COME AGAIN.

EMILY

Where is she?

JEALOUSY

I don't know.

LIZ

You are lying through your fucking teeth.

JEALOUSY

They never tell me anything, they never ... (*Starts crying.*)

LIZ

You tell me where she is or so help me I'll throw you out into that riot and let you get trampled to death this time.

They start for her. JEALOUSY freaks out.

JEALOUSY

No! Please! Joe's got her. He found out about a tape, she's in his house somewhere. That ... that's all I know, I swear.

LIZ and EMILY whip into their leather jackets and rush out the door, leaving GAZELLE standing there looking daggers at JEALOUSY Y.

GAZELLE

(*With vitriol.*) Traitor.

Blackout.

Scene Thirty-Two: Big Joey's Basement

The sound of idling motorcycles fades into silence. Up in the sky, the two pink heart/moons turn blood read as three women skulk their way across the stage, one carrying a crowbar over her shoulder. Their figures disappear into the wings. After a brief pause, there is the loud crash of a door being bashed in with the crowbar, immediately followed by the flashing on of three flashlights. Shushing each other, the three women search the room with these lights; the room is obviously Big Joey's basement. Suddenly, the beams of light fall on a woman's figure hanging from two "chains" attached to the ceiling, the woman naked and unconscious.

LIZ

Oh my god.

EMILY

(*Barely able to speak.*) Pussy ...

> *Paralysed by shock, they stand rooted. LIZ, beginning to sob, puts her arms around PUSSY's body, alleviating the pressure on PUSSY's arms.*

LIZ

Get her down, goddamn it ... get her down ...

> *EMILY and GAZELLE work the "winch" and PUSSY is gently lowered into LIZ's arms. EMILY goes to remove the shackles, but LIZ stops her with desperate eyes. With trembling fingers, LIZ removes the "shackles" from PUSSY's wrists.*

LIZ

(*Choked.*) Oh baby, baby ... it's real bad this time ...

> *Fade-out.*

Scene Thirty-Three: Outside the Casino

*Outside the Casino Royale, the motorcycle lights are
gone, the Kitchen Rhythm Band circling the "casino"
in its place, their kitchen utensils glinting in the
blood red moonlight. ZACHARY, with his rolling pin,
and PIERRE, with a barbecue fork and cheese grater,
stand centre-stage.*

PIERRE

How long you think this blockade will last, Zachary
Jeremiah?

ZACHARY

Well, two weeks so far. Who knows, lordy, lordy, lordy.

Walking by, BIG JOEY strides up to them.

BIG JOEY

So, Pierre St. Pierre. You with or against the Casino
Royale?

PIERRE

Well, as I say to anyone who cares to ask …

BIG JOEY

You toothless, useless bootleggin' old fart.

PIERRE

Bah!

BIG JOEY

And you, Zachary Jeremiah Keechigeesik, you … (*Breaks
out laughing.*) … you … you should see yourself …
running around with that rolling pin.

ZACHARY

And you should see yourself, running around like a four-
year-old tryna prove to everybody else that your little
dinky is bigger than everybody else's.

BIG JOEY

It *is* bigger than everybody else's.

ZACHARY

So what?

131

BIG JOEY

What are you doing on the women's side anyway?

ZACHARY

Well, to start with, Big Joey, I'm married to a woman. I have a mother who happens to be a woman. I have two daughters, I have ...

BIG JOEY

This casino of mine is strictly a man's business.

ZACHARY

Because you're scared shitless of women, aren't you? (*BIG JOEY stares at ZACHARY with eyes of steel.*) Scared of their ... emotions, their power ... to laugh and cry, to share love among each other without feeling ashamed, things that you have no idea how to ...

BIG JOEY

Fuck you, you fat faggot.

ZACHARY

You, Joseph Jeremiah McLeod, ashamed to feel, ashamed to love, ashamed to touch another man in case someone sees you and calls you feminine or ... faggot. (*Pause.*) Touching another human being gently—female, male—is one hell of a lot better than war, it's better than killing another man, it's better than raping a woman, it's better than brutalizing her in bed ...

> A *police car siren emerges form the distance and approaches. BIG JOEY registers this.*

BIG JOEY

Hey, this is Indian land. This casino ... they can't just come in here and ...

ZACHARY

It has nothing to do with your casino, Joe, they're coming to take you away for assault causing bodily harm, abduction and intent to murder.

BIG JOEY

You and that wolverine wife of yours can call the cops any goddamn time, and I'll still be a free man.

ZACHARY
Joe, you've got to change. Look at Gazelle Nataways.
Look how far she's come in the last few months.

BIG JOEY
Gazelle Nataways, yeah right, that bitch'll never change.
And as proof of that, Mr. Pillsbury Doughboy, she was the
one who stole that tape of Ms. Commanda's from the
Chief's and passed it on to me. The woman is gonna be
after my dick right up until the day she dies and that's
the way she is and that's way women are and there ain't
nothing you can do about it. (*Starts walking away.*) I'll be
outta that jail by tomorrow.

Scene Thirty-Four A: Outisde the Casino

Song: "Twinkle, Twinkle Little Star"

*At another point of the casino "blockade," ANNIE sits
on the ground pouring water into a row of seven
glasses, taking care that each glass contains an ever-
increasing amount of water. FRITZ THE KATZ sits
across from her.*

ANNIE
Fritz. You treat me like ... like a little pig or something.

FRITZ
No, I don't. I don't treat you like a little pig or
something. Just ... just ... gimme another chance.

ANNIE
(*Strong.*) No.

Cross-fade to ...

Scene Thirty-Four B: The Hilarium

Song: "Tansi" (reprise)

At the Hilarium, CHIEF BIG ROSE *sits in her "arm-chair" in front of the standing* WOODEN INDIAN, *a book lying open in her lap. Exhausted, she has dozed off and, suddenly, starts talking in her sleep.*

CHIEF BIG ROSE

Who ... who was it said ... said there is ... no death? That there is no such thing as dying?

In the distance, we hear the "vamp" and then the intro to the song "Tansi" and, shortly thereafter, women beginning to sing the song.

WOMEN

(*Singing.*) "Tansi, niweecheewaganuk, tansi,
Tapwee geechi kapeegee-oogeeyik;
Nimeetheeth'weeteenan tapapeeyak,
Tachimoostatak tanagamooyak ... "

A chorus of women in black leather jackets straddling "motorcycles" appears in the "distance," as through a mist, singing the song. From it, hand in hand, emerge ROSABELLA *and* ROSETTA. *They approach* CHIEF BIG ROSE. ROSETTA *takes the book from* CHIEF BIG ROSE's *lap and shows* ROSABELLA *the page where it's been open.* ROSABELLA *reads.*

ROSABELLA

(*Reading.*) "God as a Rose." (*Looks at cover.*) Dante. *The Divine Comedy.*

CHIEF BIG ROSE

(*Talking in her sleep.*) Yes. "God as a Rose." It's from my son, Tom. Down in Toronto.

Here, ROSABELLA's *speech (to* CHIEF BIG ROSE) *overlaps with* ANNIE's *(to* FRITZ, *at the casino "blockade," see above), the latter slightly in the background, like a ripple of water. The vamping rhythm of the song, "Tansi," fades slowly until it is*

gone, as is the visual of the "chorus line" of women
in black leather jackets.

ROSABELLA

(*To* CHIEF BIG ROSE.) ... it's true what they say, the Elders, the medicine people, there is no death. No death. Only a going away, to another world, another dimension of this same old ... Earth. We are still here, we will be here forever. Sixty thousand years, thirty thousand generations of us. They can kill us and they can rape us and shoot us and set our bodies on fire but we are still here, we will always be here, will never go away. Look all around you, we are here, all of us ...

ANNIE

(*To* FRITZ.) ... they say, the Elders, the medicine people, they predicted the coming of the whiteman decades, even centuries before Columbus arrived here. And they predicted the near death, the near destruction of the Indian people, but that, seven lifetimes after that arrival, five hundred years ago this year, the seventh generation of Indian people would rise up ... no, no, no, no, that's not how it Goes. Okay, okay, okay, I got it. In that seventh generation, a child will be born, who will light ... the eighth fire. And when that eighth fire is lit, the four races—white, black, yellow and red, men and women and and and the in-between people—they will find the balance. Something like that.

> *At the casino "blockade," FRITZ pauses to let ANNIE's*
> *words sink in. Then he reaches over to her for help.*
> *ANNIE gives him a teaspoon. Applying spoon to the*
> *seven glasses ANNIE has set up on the ground, FRITZ*
> *plays "Twinkle, Twinkle Little Star." As the women of*
> *Wasy begin humming the lullaby from the song,*
> *"When Children Sleep." All as ...*

135

Scene Thirty-Four C: A Hospital Room

*Song(s): "When Children Sleep" (humming only)
and "Twinkle, Twinkle Little Star" (on "water
xylophone")*

*At a "hospital room" in Sudbury, PUSSY COMMANDA
lies dying in a "bed" of flowing white sheets. At least,
she appears to be dying. Will she survive? Or will she
not? HERA is giving her a "cedar bath," wiping her
gently with a white cloth, VERONIQUE assisting her as,
close by, smoke from a braid of sweetgrass curls into
the air, LIZ sitting there tending to it. PHILOMENA,
meanwhile, sits off to the side with both arms still in
casts. At this point, the last part of ROSABELLA's
monologue emerges solo.*

Scene Thirty-Four B: The Hilarium

*Song(s): "When Children Sleep" (humming only)
and "Twinkle, Twinkle Little Star" (on "water
xylophone")*

ROSABELLA
(*To CHIEF BIG ROSE.*) ... because, you see, it's the spirit that
they can never kill. Never. Death, in the end, is a victory.
Remember that. Death. A victory.

*Pause. With ROSABELLA and ROSETTA standing to
each side of the armchair where she still sits sleeping,
CHIEF BIG ROSE speaks in her sleep, the other two
Roses speaking with her.*

THE THREE ROSES
Yes, Emily. Go for it. Ride the beast.

Scene Thirty-Five: Emily's Living Room

*In the shadows off to her side, all the previous scenes
remain sort of visible, like slides, or visions of ghosts,
as though EMILY were addressing all the women of the
world: the three Roses standing in the hilarium
looking at her (EMILY), PUSSY at the hospital with
HERA, LIZ, PHILOMENA, VERONIQUE and now ANNIE,
come to join them ...*

EMILY

... Seven rapes on this island in the past year alone, since
you guys got here: Jill Keechigeesik, short Mary Ann
Patchnose who died from internal bleeding because they
went and shoved a beer bottle up her koozie and then
broke it, Clara Jane Saunders, Twyla Hunter who ended
up in an insane asylum, Vereena Kananakeesik, Little
Dishes Frontier, Georgette Wunnumin who lost her baby
and then killed herself. How many were told they wanted
it, how many were told they asked for it, that they were to
blame? Was Zhaboonigan Peterson to blame when them
four white guys ganged up on her, rammed a screwdriver
fifty-six times into her womb, left her in the snow to
freeze and bleed to her death and then got away scott
free to do it again and again, to god knows how many
other women? Helen Betty Osborne, man, history-making
goddamn swindle. Men beating their wives with
hammers, setting them on fire, pouring acid on them.
Real manly behaviour that, huh? And then there's the
king of them all, a certain gentleman in this town named
Joseph Jeremiah McLeod. Nobody talks about it around
here, nobody stops him, everybody just turns the other
way and pretends it isn't happening, they just let him
keep doing it over and over and over again. Philomena
Moosetail, beaten to within an inch of her life. Patsy
Pegahmagahbow, raped with a crucifix by Dickie Bird
Halked as his own father, Big Joey, watched and did
nothing to stop him. Beating Lalala Lacroix senseless
with a piece of firewood, Gazelle Nataways, me, me, me,

getting Gazelle Nataways to kick me in the gut five years ago, killing my Rosetta when she was almost ready to be born. Pussy Commanda. Slicing off her nipples, watching her as she gets gang-banged by a bunch of his goons, hung up like a slab of meat at a slaughterhouse ...

When EMILY whips around, she holds ROSABELLA's shocking-red six-inch stilettos and offers them to LIZ.

Scene Thirty-Six A: Big Joey's Basement

Song: "Rio in High January"

The intro to the song, "Rio in High January," an electrifying samba, kicks in. Lights up at Big Joey's where BIG JOEY sits on the chaise longue doing calculations on a calculator.

BIG JOEY

... 4,567; 2,345; 987; 12,566; 13,003 ... (*Knock on the door.*) ... come in ... 1,332 ... and the total comes to ...

The "door" opens and an absolutely stunning LIZ JONES stands there, leaning langourously against the "door": shocking-red six-inch stilettos, skin-tight dress with a cleavage from hell, inch-long eyelashes, everything. She holds a bottle of champagne in one hand, two champagne glasses in the other.

LIZ

Got outta jail, huh, Joe? (*BIG JOEY tries to ignore her.*) And now you're counting your pennies ...

BIG JOEY

Get outta here. Go on, get outta my house.

LIZ

That's all ya got left, Joe. Pennies. You know, I got all kinds of money. LaCream money. More *mo-nay* than you ever dreamed of, Joe.

LIZ struts into the room, giving BIG JOEY a terrific eyeful.

BIG JOEY

What ... what are you doing here?

LIZ

You're washed up in Wasaychigan Hill, Joe. Let's face it,
so am I. Winter's coming on and I'm a California girl ... I
like it where it's ... hot.

*She pops the champagne cork and sneaks a powdered
drug into one of the glasses. Her words sizzle.*

You know, Puss couldn't take a man like you. Maybe
Gazelle can, who knows. But I wanna give it a try. (*She
hands him a champagne glass.*)

BIG JOEY

You're a dyke. Once a dyke, always a dyke.

LIZ

(*Purring.*) Oh, that's not true, Joe, no, no, no. Believe
me. (*Starts undressing.*) All I ever needed was a night in
the arms of the ... right man. And there's no man more
powerful, more right ... than you, Joe. Drink. Drink. It's,
ahhh, good for you. (*She drinks. Following her example, he
empties his glass.*)

BIG JOEY

(*Seduced.*) She had it coming to her, you know.

LIZ

She did, she did. (*Starts undoing his clothes.*) I'd never let
my man down, Joe.

BIG JOEY

Never? Oh, baby ...

He buries his face in her crotch.

LIZ

Have you ever wondered what the other side must look
like, Big Joey? How beautiful it must be? Soft, pink-
coloured light all around you, sweet, sweet music washing
over your skin, all your worries, all your aches and pains,
all, all gone? Have you ever wondered what the
mountains of Nepal must look like? In the rain? Or the
pampas of Argentina, the beaches of Rio?

BIG JOEY
(*Drowsy.*) Yes.

LIZ

Let's escape, let's fly, you and me, to some place far, far away,
where no one can hurt us, where no one can touch us ...

(*Starts singing.*) "Rio in high January, the beaches of Rio,
Just the thing to do this year don't you fancy Rio, Brazil;
Oh the sun and the waves of the ocean, oh yes;
I so wanna go to that city and learn how to samba and hey!
Let's call the agent who makes reservations on planes
flying south;
And we'll fly to the sunlight, oh!
We'll forget winter this winter, good-bye!
Hello to Ipanema!
I've got my suitcase, I've got all my money and
Rio in high January, the beaches of Rio ... "
(*Repeat verse.*)

> Slowly, BIG JOEY falls asleep in LIZ's arms. As LIZ
> repeats her verse and other women (in the
> background) join in with harmonies, she peels BIG
> JOEY off herself, lies him down, and starts taking off
> the last of his clothes. Pause.

Scene Thirty-Six B: The Hospital Room

Song: "Rio in High January"

*A light comes up on PUSSY, sitting up in her hospital
"bed," wrapped in a white sheet, barely alive, singing
weakly, and slowly, the slow "interlude" to the song,
"Rio in High January."*

PUSSY

(*Singing.*) "I wanna go to that place in the sun and dream
All about you and me and love;
All about you and me and the stars in the night
You and me and the moon up and above
You and me ... "

140

Scene Thirty-Six C: Big Joey's Basement

Song: "Rio in High January"

When the instrumental break starts (and the samba rhythm has returned), the woman march into Big Joey's basement—HERA, VERONIQUE, PHILOMENA, ANNIE. They help LIZ strip BIG JOEY naked and then hang him by the wrists on the two "chains" where PUSSY was found hanging earlier, BIG JOEY's back to the audience. HERA prepares a herbal poultice as the other women prepare a basin, rolls of gauze, towels, etc. and place them on the floor at his feet, all moving slowly, as in a ceremony, ROSETTA, ROSABELLA and CHIEF BIG ROSE watching from the side, all intensely aware of what is about to happen; it is as though all the women in the show have joined hands to put their seal on the ultimate pact. EMILY takes out a meat cleaver. ROSABELLA hides ROSETTA's eyes from the violence about to occur as slowly, EMILY lifts the cleaver up at BIG JOEY's crotch. And strikes. "Blood" explodes at his feet. The entire stage turns blood red, red roses exploding everywhere—on the walls, on the floor, in the sky—all as ...

Scene Thirty-Six D: The World as a Whole

Song: "Rio in High January"

The stage explodes with all the men in the show (except, of course, BIG JOEY and CREATURE) dancing on dressed in "dental floss" bikinis, Carmen-Miranda-fruit headdresses, penis-shaped maracas in hand ... and dancing a samba from hell! And singing (with the women, as the latter take BIG JOEY down gently, and wrap him in the poultice, bandages, a bathrobe, etc.)

COMPANY

(*Singing, in multi-part harmony.*) "Rio in high January, the beaches of Rio,
Just the thing to do this year don't you fancy Rio, Brazil;
Oh the sun and the waves of the ocean, oh yes;
I so wanna go to that city and learn how to samba and hey!
Let's call the agent who makes reservations on planes flying south;
And we'll fly to the sunlight, oh!
We'll forget winter this winter, good-bye!
Hello to Ipanema!
I've got my suitcase, I've got all my money and

Rio in high January, the beaches of Rio ... "
(*Repeat verse.*)

The song comes to an electrifying finish just as ...

Scene Thirty-Seven: The Main Road of Wasy

Song(s): "Kitchen Rhythm Band, "Tango" and "The Thank You Song"

CREATURE NATAWAYS stumbles to centre-stage, so drunk he can barely walk, completely dishevelled, having lost his mind.

CREATURE

(*Weepy.*) Oh, please, please, please, please, please, please get away from me, get away from me, get away from me, get away from me, get away from meeeeeee!!!!!!!
Remember, Big Joey, remember when we were little, when we were little, when we were little, little, little how we used to play in the bushes behind Lapatack St. Pierre's old corn field? ...

The two blood-red moons come to shine an eerie light on CREATURE, wandering the reserve like the madman he has become, a half-empty whisky bottle in hand, from which he takes big swigs from time to time.

... we used to chase the little field mice, the little mousies across the field and then you'd catch one and you'd take it home with you, keep it in your little box, feed it little cheeses and little garter snakes and jelly beans and stuff and you even made a little coat for one of them, remember, Big Joey?

Gradually, the sound of Zachary's Kitchen Rhythm Band can be heard away off in the distance, playing a hot samba number, in effect, the rhythm to the song, "Rio in High January."

... and you even gave him a name, you called him Lapatak. Lapatak Come Again because you didn't like Munchoos X. Come Again because he used to tease you and call you "frilly face" cuz you were so pretty, pretty as a petunia, pretty just like little Lapatak Come Again. He was so cute, that little mousie, huh, Big Joey, Lapatak Come Again was real cute? ...

ROSABELLA and ROSETTA, hand in hand, walk by him to the casino where they slowly approach the locked roulette wheel over which a pin spot now comes on.

... and you remember why Lapatak Come Again was the only one you could tell your real secret to, remember? Because your own mommy and your own daddy hated you, that's what you said, they didn't want you, you were a mistake and they were mean to you and your daddy was mean, ever mean to your mommy because ... and you wanted them dead and you didn't like them and ... (*Sings, like a child.*) "Lapatak Come Again and his coat of many colours, Lapatak Come Again and his coat of many colours, Lapatak Come Again and his coat of many colours, Lapatak Come Again and his coat of many colours, etc. ... " (*Repeat.*)

ROSABELLA "unlocks" the roulette wheel, ROSETTA spins it, and both fade into the crowd as ...

People roll "motorcycles" into position on both sides of the main road, and hang up pow wow bustles, the

Kitchen Rhythm Band marching up the aisle,
ZACHARY at the head. As all the movement swirls,
people talk among themselves.

VERONIQUE

Little Girl Manitowabi just shocked me with the news that
Chief Big Rose has decided to play a hand of blackjack
with the Trickster.

HERA

Blackjack? With Nanabush?

VERONIQUE

Yes! After they sign the treaty.

PHILOMENA

(*Now with only one arm in a cast.*) She's gambling away her
life, is what I say.

VERONIQUE

Little Girl Manitowabi insists that Nanabush is throwing
an extra moon on the table.

PHILOMENA

Madre di dios, as if we need a third moon.

HERA

They say Munchoos X. Come Again has been asked by
the Elders to remove himself from the Band Council.

An almost unrecognizable CREATURE NATAWAYS
staggers by in front of the crowd, singing insanely to
himself.

CREATURE

(*Singing.*) "Lapatak Come Again and his coat of many
colours, Lapatak Come Again and his coat of many
colours, Lapatak Come Again and his coat of many
colours, etc. ... " (*Repeat.*)

Shocked, people murmur to each other. We can just
catch snippets of what they are saying.

COMPANY

(*Gasp.*) Big Joey this and Big Joey that and Big Joey this
and Big Joey that and blah, blah, blah ...

HERA

And I, for one, believe every word of it.

VERONIQUE

And what's more, they say Munchoos X. Come Again's bank account in Switzerland has been frozen.

PHILOMENA

So much for Jealousy Y. Come Again's "little excursions" to Paree and Rome and New York and ooh-la-la, la-la …

VERONIQUE

Is it true what Black Lady Halked was telling me at the bingo that Zachary Jeremiah Keechigeesik plans to run for Vice-Chief to replace that horrible Munchoos? Or have my ears been playing tricks on me again?

ANNIE

You sure Pussy's gonna be okay for singing tonight?

EMILY

Oh, take a valium, of course, she's gonna sing.

CREATURE staggers past again. And again, people murmur in shock.

CREATURE

(*Singing.*) "Lapatak Come Again and his coat of many colours, Lapatak Come Again and his coat of many colours, Lapatak Come Again and his coat of many colours, etc. … " (*Repeat.*)

COMPANY

(*Gasp.*) Gazelle Nataways this and Gazelle Nataways that and Gazelle Nataways this and Gazelle Nataways that and blah, blah, blah …

An embittered GAZELLE NATAWAYS passes by and curses the crowd.

GAZELLE

(*Shrieks.*) Atim ootagayuk. (*Walks off.*)

CHIEF BIG ROSE comes walking up the aisle wearing her pink Indian chief headdress, her famous silver hammer in one hand, a scroll of paper (the "Treaty") in the other. CREATURE passes her, watches her for a

moment, and then continues singing as he staggers
off into the audience and disappears.

CREATURE

(*Singing.*) "Lapatak Come Again and his coat of many
colours, Lapatak Come Again and his coat of many
colours, Lapatak Come Again and his coat of many
colours, etc. ... " (*Repeat.*)

ZACHARY

Chief Big Rose, he's late ...

CHIEF BIG ROSE

She, Zachary Jeremiah, she, not he ...

ZACHARY

Quite right, quite right. *She*'s late. People are starting to
think that you cancelled him, ah, *her*, too.

CHIEF BIG ROSE

Does a bear shit in the woods?

PHILOMENA

Yes.

> *Throwing PHILOMENA a withering look, CHIEF BIG*
> *ROSE gets up on a box and, raising her hammer,*
> *addresses the raucous assembly.*

CHIEF BIG ROSE

My people. (*No one pays attention.*) Can I have your attention, please. (*Crowd continues babbling.*) Can I have your
attention, please. (*Still no response. Getting angry, she swings*
her hammer and bangs VERONIQUE over the head by accident,
continuing unawares.) Will you please let me talk?
(*VERONIQUE reels about for the remainder of the scene.*) Thank
you. Now, as you know, I've cancelled Elvis Presley and
invited Nanabush in his place to come and officially open
the new "Casino *Un*-Royale," which will now truly belong
to the people as it was always intended to be, *and* sign the
Treaty giving the entire *universe* back to the Indians, an
agreement which I have been postponing and postponing
and postponing because you know how I just *love* to
cancel things ...

*Suddenly, a new murmur ripples through the crowd.
It parts and PIERRE, still black of face from the
exploded grenade, comes wheeling a brand new
"stove" on a dolly, a cheese grater and egg beater tied
to his waist. The stove is covered with pink ribbons
and roses. And PIERRE himself wears a dress and
heels. He wheels the stove right up to VERONIQUE,
throws his cheese grater and egg beater to ZACHARY
and stands in front of the still-reeling VERONIQUE, his
chest puffed out with pride.*

PIERRE

Happy birthday, little bag.

*VERONIQUE grabs her weak heart and faints dead
away. With one incredibly graceful swoop, PIERRE
catches VERONIQUE in his arms. Holding her there,
halfway to the ground, he throws a look over at
ZACHARY, who stands waiting in front of his "band."*

Hit it, Zach.

*Making a great ceremony of it all, ZACHARY passes
his rolling pin to LIZ JONES.*

ZACHARY

Ms. Jones?

*Proudly—and tongue in cheek—LIZ turns to the
Kitchen Rhythm Band and starts to conduct it with
Zachary's rolling pin. And, with great skill, the band
plays the same tango we heard in Big Joey's basement
in Act One. And PIERRE proceeds to drag and throw
his comatose wife about on the dirt road, as if she
were a rag doll, doing this amazingly graceful, and
stylish, tango. Unseen by anyone, CREATURE
NATAWAYS enters through the audience and, from a
distance, slowly points a handgun directly at CHIEF
BIG ROSE's forehead.*

CHIEF BIG ROSE

(*Cheering the ST. PIERRES.*) Bravo! Bravo, bravo, bravo!

*A shot rings out. CHIEF BIG ROSE's headdress is
suddenly splattered with "blood," right at the
forehead. Silence. Stillness.*

*Pin spot on EMILY's shocked face, the only light which
stays on consistently through the next series of scenes.*

*First echo of gunshot: a vision of MUNCHOOS X.
sitting on a lawn chair smoking a cigar and
drinking champagne as, before him on the "lawn,"
JEALOUSY Y. weeps and plays her cello.*

*Second echo: in his basement, BIG JOEY kneels facing
the wall, naked, as GAZELLE NATAWAYS, dressed as a
dominatrix, whips his back with a cat-o-nine tails.*

*Third echo: his BODYGUARD behind him, LUCIANO
BOCCIA kneels in "church" praying to a crucifix
hanging on a wall.*

*At centre-stage, CHIEF BIG ROSE, gunshot through her
forehead, blood streaming down her face, collapses
backwards into the crowd.*

*At first, it sounds like wolves in the distance, howling
at the moon. But it is actually women, lamenting,
crying out, their Cree and English weaving in and
out of each other. And during their lament, EMILY
slowly walks to her living room couch to sit there
paralysed by shock.*

WOMEN
Igwani! Igwani eewaniya-ak kimisinow! Igwani eewaniya-
ak kitoogimaminow! Tansi itigwee igwa pascatch
keetootamak! Tansi itigwee igwa pascatch keetootamak!
... Lost! Lost! We have lost our sister! We have lost our
dearly beloved Rose! What are we to do? Oh, what are we
to do? ...

*As these voices fade into first low moans and whispers
and then silence, a low drum beat begins, as though
from a great distance. Slowly, the crowd moves
forward, carrying CHIEF BIG ROSE's body to downstage centre. The production band joins the drum
beat with the intro to "The Thank You Song."*

*In her pin spot, EMILY slowly brings her head up, her
face wet with tears as, from somewhere in the crowd,
ROSABELLA begins to sing and, as she sings, emerges
from that crowd hand in hand with ROSETTA.*

ROSABELLA

(*Singing.*) "When day begins to sigh,
And Earth turns to ask her why;
Then man will lift up a hand,
To send out the sound of the cry,
Oh the cry of the lonely,
Oh the cry of the lost,
To the sun and the sky,
Who will hear him not."

> *As EMILY goes into the second verse, she stands up
> and the women slowly move to their positions beside
> their "motorcycles," putting on their black leather
> jackets. The men recede into the background, though
> the best of them are certainly there.*

EMILY

(*Singing.*) "When night falls upon us all,
And stars pierce the heart of the sky,
Then man will lift up a hand,
To send out the sound of the cry,
Oh the cry of the lonely,
Oh the cry of the lost,
To the moon and the stars,
Who will hear him not."

> *EMILY, LIZ and PUSSY sing the chorus—in unison—
> with ROSABELLA and ROSETTA, during which
> ROSABELLA and ROSETTA slowly come up the aisle of
> "motorcycles" and pow wow dancing bustles towards
> CHIEF BIG ROSE's body.*

EMILY/LIZ/PUSSY/ROSABELLA/ROSETTA

(*Singing.*) "You were the one who had answers for,
Questions that we in our need would have,
And for all of this we would like to say,
Thank you for the love you gave."

During the instrumental break here (sax solo), the
"motorcycles" move into V-formation (facing the
audience), with CHIEF BIG ROSE's body at the tip of
the V. ROSABELLA and ROSETTA each take a hand of
CHIEF BIG ROSE. CHIEF BIG ROSE's ghost *rises.*

ROSABELLA and ROSETTA first escort CHIEF BIG ROSE's
spirit to the "motorcycle" at the tip of the V, help her
get on it, and then go to straddle the two "bikes"
immediately behind and flanking her. Other women
are now straddling the "motorcycles" to the rear,
leaving the ones immediately behind ROSABELLA and
ROSETTA vacant for now. Behind these vacant
"motorcycles" sit HERA, VERONIQUE and the rest of the
women. Only LIZ, PUSSY and EMILY remain standing.

EMILY

(*Singing.*) "When love ceases to exist,
When breath soft begins to die;
Then man will lift up a hand,
To send out the sound of the cry ... "

> *ROSABELLA joins her, in harmony, for the next four*
> *lines.*

EMILY/ROSABELLA

"Oh the cry of the lonely,
Oh the cry of the lost,
To the Earth and the sky,
Who will hear him not."

> *As they sing the next statement of the chorus (now in*
> *multi-part harmony), LIZ and PUSSY climb aboard the*
> *vacant "motorcycles" behind ROSABELLA and*
> *ROSETTA, leaving only EMILY standing now.*

EMILY/LIZ/PUSSY/ROSABELLA/ROSETTA

(*Singing.*) "You were the one who had answers for,
Questions that we in our need would have,
And for all of this we would like to say,
Thank you for the love you gave."

> *As the entire company joins in—in multi-part*
> *harmony—with the next two (and final) statements*

*of the chorus (each repeat getting increasingly
ornate), EMILY gets on the last vacant "bike" and the
lights work to give the following miraculous illusion:*

*Gradually, the "motorcycles" sprout wings (i.e. the
pow wow dancing bustles held to one side) and the
trio of Roses begins to rise in a mist. On the backdrop
away upstage are projected images of first the night
lights of Wasy as seen from the air, then Manitoulin
Island, then Sudbury, then Toronto, then New York,
then the globe of the world as it floats in space, then
the stars and, finally, an empty night sky punctuated
only by two pink moons shaped like hearts. The spirits
of all these women—goddesses now—are escorting,
flying, the souls of all three Roses into the spirit world
as, from a "distance," they look like geese in their bi-
annual migration—they are geese in their bi-annual
migration. As the song ends and the lights begin
fading into blackout, a third pink heart "rises" slowly
to the sky to join the two already there. And the Earth
now has three moons, moons made of the hearts of
three Native women named Rose: ROSETTA (small
moon), ROSABELLA (medium) and CHIEF BIG ROSE
(large).*

*Lit by a pin spot, ROSETTA stands at centre-stage
down, hands hidden behind her back, all the women
behind her frozen into their silhouettes. Smiling
impishly at the audience, she reveals the object she's
been hiding behind her back—her "Rosetta biker
doll"—and, hopping off the stage, goes "play-flying"
the doll up an aisle and out the theatre, giggling
happily all the way and leaving in her wake a theatre
echoing and echoing with little girl laughter.*

All fades into darkness. And silence.

*And in that darkness and silence, a heartbeat
thumps. And the Earth breathes ...*

The End.

Should Only Native Actors
Have the Right to Play Native Roles?

Deep in my Cree heart of hearts, I had two millennium projects on the go, though this only in hindsight. One was for the year 2000, the other for the year 2001, and this just to make sure I had the right year for the actual beginning of this brand new, and incredibly exciting, millennium. Those two projects? For the year 2000, an English-language production, in Toronto, of the third play in what I call my "Rez Septology," a play called *Rose*. And for the year 2001, the Japanese-language premiere, in Tokyo, of the second play in that septology, a play called *Dry Lips Oughta Move To Kapuskasing*. And this is how the two projects affected me and my life:

When it dawned on me, one cloudy day, that my career as a playwright had been destroyed by political correctness, I just about died. I wanted to throw myself under a subway train and just call it a day. I was horrified! After all that work? After all those years of struggle and of hope and of prayer and of pain and of tears and of more struggle, against odds that were impossible to begin with? But how can it be? How can the voice of a playwright be silenced? By a method so brutally effective as political correctness? In a country supposedly as civilized as Canada? Questions like this, and others like them, resounded through my brain over and over and over again. As they do to this day. Permit me, therefore, to start off with the "backdrop" before I go into "the projects," please:

First of all, I don't happen to have the good fortune of coming from a city such as Montreal or Vancouver or Toronto or Ottawa or New York or any other major city where educational (and employment) opportunities, right from age one, are virtually unlimited (believe me, you can be a movie star by age one in such cities!). And I don't come from a city where English (or French) is the language of the day. I come, instead, from one of the tiniest, most remote, most inaccessible, most underprivileged and most troubled Indian reserves in the country, Brochet, Manitoba, population 700, one thousand five hundred kilometres directly north of Winnipeg (further north than Churchill but on the opposite side of the province). I come from a place where the language spoken is Cree. AND Dene, incidentally; because we are located so far north, we spill over into the land of such sub-arctic peoples as the Dene, cousins (linguistically speaking) to the Navajo and other southwest Native nations. In fact, to fly from Toronto (my home until recently) to Brochet costs more than a ticket from Toronto to Sydney, Australia or to Rio de Janeiro. To fly home to visit my family (which I do regular as clockwork), I could fly from Toronto to London, England and back—three times each way—for the same amount of money, easy. No jumping in a taxi or a car or on a bus or a train or a "seat-sale" seat on a plane from Toronto to Vancouver for the likes of us, not to go have lunch with Mom, not to go to a funeral. Plane ticket prices for Canada's northerners? Brutal. Brutal, brutal, brutal. And that's just the distance barrier, never mind the linguistic. For Cree is as different from English as English is from Cantonese; not one shred of resemblance exists. In fact, the two languages are often completely at odds with each other. In one language, just for instance, God is male, in the other, female. And that's just the start ...

So along comes this little Indian boy from one such remote northern Native community and into the big, big city of Toronto and he dares to dream of a career in the theatre, or, at the very least, in the world of Canadian letters. Fat chance, baby! Forget it.

He doesn't listen. He goes ahead anyway. "No matter how they laugh, let them laugh. I can do it," he says to himself. And he puts his shoulder to the grindstone, as they say in the movies.

People always say that *The Rez Sisters* was my first play. That's not true. It's not true at all. It may have been my first play to be successful with the general public. But there were five plays that came before that, every one of them self-produced, with money from my very own pocket. And some of these plays were awful, some of them were good, at least two of them were very, very good.

But only with *The Rez Sisters* did my work suddenly, finally get noticed by, as I say, a wider public. By which time, I was almost forty. And what I had to go through to get those first five plays self-produced, you don't even wanna know! How do you make money standing with your back against a wall in some big city, downtown back alley? Late, late at night? Guess.

When it came to that "first" play, however—and I speak here about *The Rez Sisters*, which, in fact, was my sixth—it was the fall of 1986. In those days, of course, you could have counted the number of professional Native actors in this country on the fingers of one hand alone. In my wildest dreams—keeping in mind that my work was totally unknown then—I dared to write this play for "them," meaning those four or five professional Native actors then in existence. The reason? I adored them. I just absolutely adored these people AND their work. They were my heroes. They kept my dreams alive.

So then it came to the casting of the show. Finally, my play was going to get done! I was so excited I could hardly sleep at nights. So then I approached them, these Native actors, for you see, as always, I was the producer, again, or at least in this case, one of two co-producers, god bless the other co-producer, may he rest in peace. These Native actors, however, they all said "no." They were all too busy working on other projects, many of them on Native subject matter written by—horrors!—white people! I pleaded with them and pleaded with them and pleaded with them but, still, they said "no." God bless them and their courageous careers but they made me cry. They made me want to give up and die.

So what choice did I have? Either I forget the play and kill myself. OR I go right ahead and hire—horrors!—white actors! Which is what I did, exactly. And these white actors, they were SO generous, they were so kind, so supportive, so confidence-generating that, with their help—as with that of those Native actors who did say "yes," god bless them—I simply bloomed. The play opened. The play was successful. And it has never really stopped playing ever since, somewhere in the world, giving continued employment to many, many, many actors both Native and non-Native. As it will do probably forever—your grand-children will be playing in *The Rez Sisters*!—something that would NEVER have happened IF not for the help of extremely generous people who happened NOT to be Native, actors who happened to be white!

Several years later, I experienced a similar situation. This time, it was with a play called *Rose*. Again I wrote it for Native actors—of which, by this time (1991), there were many more—actors whom I absolutely adored, whose work I absolutely adored. And again, for some strange reason, they said "no." They were NOT interested. I couldn't get them interested. If their objective was to make me cry, then they were certainly utterly successful.

So then I waited ten years. Ten years! And by this time, I'm almost fifty years old, okay? Until some incredibly generous non-Native person comes along and offers to produce it, albeit in a university setting, that is, a non-professional (i.e., non-paying) setting. I was thrilled. I was so thrilled I could have danced myself to shreds!

So then they went to work on it, this group of "white kids," none of whom was older than twenty-five. And they worked. And they worked and they worked and they worked and they worked. Never seen a group of people work SO hard. And with so much faith and so much conviction and so much love. It was a blessing from heaven to be sitting there beside them, to be in the same room as them. They glowed, they glowed like lightbulbs. You've never seen people so happy, so high. And by the time the show opened, you couldn't get a ticket; it had been sold out way before opening; hundreds of people were turned away. On virtually no advertising; it all happened by word of mouth. And, to me—as to most people who saw it—the production was FANTASTIC! It was rich, it was beautiful, it was spectacular, it was moving, it was … miraculous! Not perfect, perhaps, but pretty gall-darned good.

But these were the things about this experience that most struck me, that most stayed with me:

1) Not one of these actors got paid; they were students; in fact, because they were students of the drama programme at the University of Toronto, they were paying for the experience through their tuition fees which, if I understand correctly, can be as much as $8,000 a year at that particular institution. Pardon me—ONE of those actors DID get paid, a little girl we needed who, of course (being little), came from outside the drama programme.

And she, by the way—and god bless her—was the only performer in that production who was Native. But how many Native actors do YOU know who would be willing to pay $8,000 to be in a show? Any show? That question stunned me.

2) All the other performers? Well, we had French-Canadians and Anglo-Canadians and Dutch-Canadians and Polish-Canadians and Ukrainian-Canadians and Jewish-Canadians and Peruvian-Canadians and Lebanese-Canadians and Portuguese-Canadians and god only knows what else! And none of them had ever met a Native person, up until then. They pretty well all came from the city of Toronto, or somewhere very close by (such as Barrie, or Sudbury) so they had never, ever been privy to any even remotely "Native experience" in their lives. Now, for the first time, in their third year of university, at ages 21 to 25, here they were getting this heavy-duty immersion course in "Native Studies," meaning Native culture, Native history, Native spirituality, Native language—they were learning to speak Cree, for god's sake, something you can't get Cree kids to do these days!—Native art, Native music, and, just generally, Native life in this country, today. And you know what? They all fell in love with it. Now, as the direct result of such an experience, what they have for Native culture and people and languages is endless respect, even awe. And love. And what's more, they will pass that knowledge and that love and respect—and wisdom—on to their children and their grandchildren and their great grandchildren, etc., etc., etc. ... The experience changed their lives. And both communities—Native AND non-Native—will benefit from it, both in the long term AND permanently.

The experience certainly changed MY life. It shocked me. The shock? That generosity and kindness and love know no racial boundaries. And that, contrariwise, UNgenerosity and lack of kindness and just plain cruelty ALSO know no racial boundaries. Coming out of *Rose*, I ended up with the immense gift of, minimum, 30 gorgeous, fantastically kind new friends, people whose friendship and generosity—and laughter—I will cherish right up until the day I die.

And the icing on the cake? A show was born that otherwise would never have been born, that otherwise would have died forever. A show was born that will give useful, meaningful, enriching employment—and enjoyment—to many, many people for many, many years. Like, I say, the whole thing was a shock. And it took ten years!

One more story before I close off on my point, the story, that is, of my second "millennium project," so-called. As it turns out, I'm writing this from Japan, specifically Tokyo, where the Japanese-language production of another play of mine, *Dry Lips Oughta Move To Kapuskasing*, just opened.

It was awesome. And, again, it wasn't so much the production—which was absolutely stunning! Imagine, if you will, the Seven Samurai doing *Dry Lips* ... —that moved me so much as the generosity of the cast and crew, Japanese every one of them. That generosity, that kindness, that largeness of heart, just astonished me. It made me cry. To be the beneficiary of kindness on that scale is a gift one could easily die for. As a result of just that one project, I now have a hundred friends, easy, in Japan. For the rest of my life! I LOVE Tokyo!

And again, none of these people had ever met a Native person—well, two had, but ... —much less knew anything about Native culture first hand. By the end of the six-week rehearsal process, however, some of them were speaking Cree AND some Ojibway. And let me tell you, to hear your own Native tongue being spoken with a Japanese accent is a bittersweet experience indeed. (I mean, come on, folks! To be unilingual in a language that's not even your own? If the Japanese can learn Cree, YOU can learn Ojibway!) And, again, these people will pass their respect for Native people and culture on to their children, their grand-children, their great great grandchildren, etc., etc., etc. ... The experience changed their lives. It changed mine.

The one question I kept being asked over and over? How does it feel to have Japanese actors playing Native parts? (In the afore-mentioned Canadian production of *The Rez Sisters*, it was more like, "how dare these two white women STEAL Native parts from Native actors!" Well, good grief! The show would never have been born without them in the first place!) Anyway, my answer to the question in Japan was this:

1) These Japanese actors, they're human beings, for god's sake. What they are, first, foremost and last, is real-life, flesh-and-blood human beings with feelings, human beings who happen to be

incredibly talented. And incredibly generous. If they hadn't agreed to do it, it would never, EVER have happened.

2) To me, saying that only Native actors have the right to play Native roles—on stage, anyway, as opposed to film, which is another thing entirely and not at all what I'm talking about here— well, that's like saying only Italian actors have the right to play in *Romeo and Juliet*, or only Danish actors have the right to play in *Hamlet*, or only Spanish actors have the right to play in *Blood Wedding*. It would be like saying to someone like Canadian film- maker Atom Egoyan, "you have the right to work with Armenian actors only," which, of course, would automatically bring his career to a standstill; it would destroy it, it would kill it, right there on the spot. Or as I asked, one sunny day, a respected, much- admired Jewish theatre artist, "how would you like to work with no one but Jews for the rest of your life?" You could almost see his hair stand on end; the very thought horrified him.

My argument with someone else at that same summer gathering? "Theatre is about illusion, art is about magic; the better the illusion, the better the magic, the more profound the experience." Besides, working in a situation of cultural, ethnic and linguistic diversity can be the most empowering, most liberating, most exhilarating experience in anyone's life. Working in a pressure cooker environment by comparison? Working in the context of a "ghetto" of any kind whatsoever, be that ghetto Native or black or French or English or Jewish or female or male or gay or ... ? Remember the expression, "familiarity breeds contempt"? Well, only too frequently, such a working environment can only mean THAT kind of disaster. Or one of plain, out-and-out hatred. And hatred, as who doesn't know, kills and kills completely. It kills relationships, it kills communities, it kills love. Look at what the Argentinians did TO EACH OTHER during the so-called "dirty war" of the 1970s. Look at what the Spanish did TO EACH OTHER during the Spanish Civil War. Look at what the Chileans have done TO EACH OTHER. Look at the Irish in Northern Ireland. Look at the Balkans, at Cambodia in the '80s, at Haiti, at Rwanda, etc., etc., etc. ... Does anybody out there actually want to live like that? Internally directed hatred, internally directed violence—which, in essence, is what civil war is—well, there is nothing more destructive, we all know that. Diversity! What we all need is diversity! What we all need, desperately, is room to breathe! That's what makes Canada work as a society: precisely its diversity. If we—all of us—were Cree, I would have had my head macheted off a long, long time ago!

All by way of saying the following: "Only Native actors have the right to play Native roles?" Music to Native actors' ears, perhaps, yes, god bless them. But death to a Native playwright's career. Because chances are that the show will NEVER, ever get done. No producer in the country has balls that size, balls big enough, that is to say, of going against the political grain. Not today. Not tomorrow.

Stop it, you people! It's killing us!

Myself, I had to move out of the country, finally. I could no longer live there, not really. I kind of live, well … all over the world now. I go where I can find the work. Because I certainly am NOT finding it in my own country. I go where I can find the kindness, I go where I can find the generosity, I go where I can find the friendship and support. The working situation in Canada, for someone like me? Well, it has simply become unworkable. I find it stultifying, asphyxiating. I CAN'T work under such artificial constraints. No one can. Sooner or later, it will drive you crazy. Not to mention kill your imagination. AND your career. All as you watch, with envious eyes, the careers of your non-Native playwright colleagues (whom you love) bloom like a garden everywhere around you …

It seems to me that what we have here are two distinct choices: a) either we cast a show politically correctly (meaning only Native actors play Native parts) and the show never, ever gets produced (trust me; I waited ten years for *Rose* to happen, more for others which will NEVER get done), or b) cast it any way you want, in whatever way you can afford it budget-wise (plane tickets are a source of money, trust me), let the show be born, let the show become successful, and THEN it will live on forever to employ many, many more actors, Native and otherwise, for many, many more years. And the upshot of the latter arrange-[ment]? Having Native and non-Native actors working side by side [on it]? There is no better healing agent for bringing two only-[appar]ently disparate, disharmonious communities together.

And, in the process, making our country an even better, richer, healthier country than it is already.

The life of an artist is so incredibly challenging, after all, a Native artist's most especially, in Canada today, or anywhere in the world. Everywhere you turn, insurmountable obstacles meet you square in the face. Everywhere you turn, events, or people, conspire to bring you down, to destroy you. What those artists need, and need most desperately, is as much breathing space as you can give them; what they need is to be given all the freedom you can give them, the freedom to create, the freedom to employ, the freedom to fly with their souls and their imaginations. Don't hold them down. Don't shoot them down. You will kill them. Or drive them away. They need all the help they can possibly acquire. They've already almost killed themselves just to get to where they are today.

Someone said to me one day: "Artists are here to break down barriers, not to create them." So, myself, I've moved away. I've left my own country, to continue helping to break down barriers in whatever way I still can, at my age, in the only way that I know how, and to have a good time doing it. The thing is, I can do that. I can take it. I've had, as they say in the business, my "fifteen minutes of fame." Enough already. I've been very, very lucky (not to mention being the beneficiary of extraordinary teachers, absolutely extraordinary parents and many dear, dear friends). And I've moved on, to other things. I have had, after all, no choice.

The sad thing is this: what about the next generation of Native playwrights? Will they, too, one day find themselves standing on that subway platform—late, late at night, stoned, drunk out of their skulls, not a penny in their pockets, no future in sight—and those long, silvery tracks down below gleaming up at them in manner most, most enticing?

* This essay was published in *Prairie Fire* Vol. 22, No. 3, Autumn